AF862230

Know RELIEF FOR THE FAMILY

Tried and True Methods for Helping an Addicted Child.

DR. PETER A. BUTKINS

DISCLAIMER STATEMENT

The information presented through this publication is for educational purposes only. Any information provided should not be interpreted as a substitute for clinical evaluation or treatment. It is definitely not intended to provide or confirm a diagnosis, nor is any claim made as to the effectiveness of any treatment or product. Seek the advice of a licensed practitioner if you have specific problems. Users of this publication are advised to rely on their own training, education and experience, and exercise due diligence and common sense in selecting a practitioner, product, or service. MyFreedomQuest, Inc. shall have no liability whatsoever for direct or indirect, special or consequential damages relating in any way to the use of information provided by MyFreedomQuest, Inc. or any of its associates, or resulting from any defects of failure of this information provided by its associates.

For information, please contact:

MyFreedomQuest, Inc.
C/o Dr. Peter A. Butkins
378 CenterPointe Circle Suite #1272
Altamonte Springs, FL 32701

Created in the United States of America

FOREWORD

Very few alcoholics and drug addicts (about 5%) ever admit they have a problem, much less do anything about it. My brother is blessed to be in that 5% group. He is one of the people you meet in life who "walks what he talks". He has written this book to reach the other 95%, as well as encourage those already in recovery programs.

I've seen him go through the seasons of life and enjoy the good times and felt the hurt during the bad times. Interestingly, most of the truly good and joyous times have occurred during his "season of recovery".

He has a lot of life's battle scars and his share of healed wounds. We all do to varying degrees. Peter knows, practices, and teaches 12-step recovery. He knows how to help you if you'll simply have a teachable heart.

Learn from his experiences and seriously take to heart the words of wisdom in these pages. They can literally save your life, or change it for the better at the very least

- Bob Butkins

Know RELIEF FOR THE FAMILY

DEDICATION

I dedicate this book to my wonderful daughter, Elizabeth,

with hopes that she won't have to suffer from such an uninvited,

unasked for and treacherous disease as addiction.

PREFACE

My motivation for writing this book began many years ago. It began with a student's overdose when I was teaching high school. This shocking event gave me a simple and basic understanding of addiction. It can be fatal! My book ends on a better note. It can be treated successfully!!!

I have lived over four decades watching addiction destroy good people. My license in marriage and family therapy has been invaluable as I have treated hundreds of families afflicted with addiction and hundreds not afflicted with addiction. In addition, I have been 'drawn' to the field of addiction treatment because I have been 'drawn' into addiction myself. More importantly, I have seen many people get sober and clean with hard work, the co-alcoholic and co-addict heal from the pain of addiction and the problems inherent in addictive families get better with treatment. As a result, I have had and still have much hope.

There is much conflict and mixed research about addiction treatment methods. However, I believe in my methods that are Tried and True. Treatment works. Our job is to get the adolescent addict to treatment. My methods work because I know that the problem lies in getting the family 'on board' to influence the child before all get too discouraged. This is why I wrote this book.

I have my license in mental health counseling. As a result, I have been able to help many individuals who have had a stress-related disorder, a 'problem in living' or one of the more severe mental illnesses. I also have much expertise in diagnosing co-occurring disorders that sometimes are a contributing relapse factor. I am a certified addiction professional (CAP) and have treated many who have recovered with the help of twelve-step programs and an intact, healthy family also in recovery and have seen this work the best.

I have a background in testing and research from Niagara University, the University of Central Florida and the University of Florida. This has helped me in evaluating treatment effectiveness, an area that is important for addiction treatment.

This combination of chemical dependence, marriage and family and mental health training and experience has been invaluable as it has allowed me to see all facets of treatment of the addictive person. I believe that we in the addictions field need to be trained in all of these areas and disciplines and also have a background in research in order to treat people ethically and effectively. This attitude of professionalism is necessary when working with families especially where there is a child who has been affected. It is important to know how to be open-minded enough to differentiate between addiction and mental health issues, use the treatment and methods that work as well and know when to use medication and when not to use medication. This ability to assess and treat addiction has given me the utmost hope for treatment and my wish is to pass this hope and success to you and your family.

I have watched families and our country suffer ever since the breakup of the family. Since the 1960's the attitude of many in this country and other countries has slowly moved towards acceptance and even approval of alcohol and drug use to include legalization of harmful substances. This, along with the proliferation of divorce, has led to irresponsible parenting and parent-less children. Fathers leave and don't come back. Mothers give birth to drug addicted children. Parents teach children that they are victims because of past wrongs. Addicted people do not forgive. They pass it on in more ways than one.

I have searched 'high and low' to come up with a simple way to tell you the way out. I have studied and given much thought into a way to explain, educate and motivate you to take action – the action needed to defuse this time bomb and lead your family into prosperity for generations to come. I want to lead us from this compulsion of enabling 'sick (not bad) behavior' by supporting cute, spoiled addicts and shunning great leaders who speak of a Higher Entity without drama and emotionalism and with balance and humility. We have to begin to support altruistic capitalism and achievement and country pride and courage and family values and education and higher standards in education and politics, sport and entertainment.

I do not foster censorship of anyone or anything. I support empowerment and healthy pride in self, family and country. This is the way we get our kids sober and clean – by developing and using great character. This is about our children, both the addicts and the ones who are not affected. IT'S ABOUT STOPPING ADDICTION FOR FUTURE GENERATIONS – FOR OUR CHILDREN. This is my motivation for this book. I want it to be your motivation.

I have intentionally been repetitious as the material I present in this book bears repetition. There is an emphasis on developing a different mindset, a new way to look at parenting in an addictive family that symbolizes 'uncharted waters' for most parents. There has to be a change in longstanding thoughts and thus the development of a new set of beliefs or else this problem will continue to perpetuate throughout future generations. What I'm asking you to do is trust this new process and discard your old ways of parenting that work so well in a 'normal' family where there is no addiction. This is easier than it may seem. No one wants this problem.

There are limitations to this writing. First of all, there are no guarantees that anyone will get sober and clean. There never are. However, after many decades of studying this disease, I can assure you that I have come up with a great model and plan to help you redirect you child back to the success that you have modeled for him. Second, the study of the disease of addiction is not an exact science. It is comprised of many parts to include biological, psychological, social and spiritual. The mental health and chemical dependence fields are divided on the definition, causes, symptoms, and solution to this problem. I am not! The traditional approach of empowerment inherent in many counseling disciplines is usually the last approach that helps an addict. This is because the untreated addict, who thinks he is God and in control of his addiction, will misinterpret empowerment for control and think that he is in control of his addiction. The psychological model is not valid as psychological problems may trigger use in some addicts but the disease causes psychological problems every time in all addicts. The moral model is not valid as many addicts are morally fit before they use.

Surrender and being teachable are the directions he must take in order to recover. Our job is to get him desperate enough to want to do this. One of the reasons children do not get sober and clean is because the parents give up if the child is not motivated at first. We need to use our combined intelligence and efforts to bring your child to acceptance. Recovery is a process and we need to persevere when they are stuck. It's that simple. (For the purpose of this study, for ease in writing, "he" will be used as the gender instead of using both genders. Addiction will refer to alcohol and/ or drug dependence.)

Lastly, while I speak of the effectiveness of the twelve-step programs, I do not represent nor is this book or my treatment affiliated with any twelve-step program; this writing is not the opinion of any twelve-step program.

ACKNOWLEDGMENTS

This book is the result of many people delivering many messages of recovery for many years. Charla B. is the biggest inspiration. Without her message, I would have been left in the dark. God rest her soul! Many thanks to Dan Clark, my most influential boss, who led us to success in Niagara Falls, 'way back when'. Milton Robinson was the best 'shrink' I ever met; next was Harry Goldfarb. Dr. Larry Loesch from the University of Florida who gave me another chance told me I was an expert on addiction and to him I owe a debt of gratitude for his inspiration.

I owe a lot to my clients who have taught me so much.

Richard Pandolfi inspired me to start this book. Chris Cranias was also influential as he impressed upon me the gravity of the 'oxy' problem in Florida. Both have done 'wonders' with their boys. Both have stopped the disease in this generation. Numerous recovering people have taught me how to think. I owe God and them my recovery.

Linda M. reviewed this writing and inspired me as did my friend, Bob.

My family has always been there and that has always made the difference. Thanks to my sisters, Val and Tina and my brothers, Bob and Jack.

Without my wonderful daughter, Elizabeth, I would never have written anything of meaning.

My Higher Power has made all possible.

My wonderful mother has been a great inspiration. I owe her and me and God my character. My sisters, Tina and Val have raised wonderful families. What's better than that?

INTRODUCTION

KNOW RELIEF FOR THE FAMILY

How to help your child get sober and clean

This is a book about hope. Hope for your child and your family. At times in my long career, I thought it was useless to treat young adults. I stayed away from treating this population until about ten years ago after I again became inspired. Since then, I've worked on family theory, strategy and techniques that work. I have found that treatment incorporating the family can work if the family will take charge under the supervision of a licensed marriage and family therapist who is also a certified addiction professional with a mental health license and over 45 years of experience in all of these fields. That's an invitation to join me.

My model and techniques work as long as your child is still bonded with you. His age does not matter as much as the relationship that you have with him. I have worked with many, many children in their twenties and thirties who are still relying on their parents to help them. This is workable. You are the "leverage" and we need to use this to "bring him to decision" and either slowly or faster get him to recovery.

In the following pages, I'm going to introduce you to an approach to treatment that works. My model is based on many years, many people, much success and much pain and loss. I have designed a personalized approach that is called RELAXED, a seven step procedure that helps you to personalize treatment based on your child. This model incorporates counseling styles that are appropriate to your child's age, maturity, drug and/or alcohol abuse severity and his personality. The approach will be tailored to his level of addiction and accompanying problems. His "downfall" will be assessed to see just what will influence him, to whom he will listen, how to approach him verbally and when and in what tone to talk to him. I have included many models, systems and examples of ways to counteract his desire to continue using drugs and alcohol. My hope is that, by studying this book, you will have the tools to help your child escape from the chains of addiction. I wrote it as though you were going to do this within the family or with the help of a therapist and a twelve-step program. I know that few parents will attend Al-Anon so I wanted to show you the way to recovery with and without this. With Al-Anon your success will be exponentially higher.

There are things that you have to do but it is so much easier than living with addiction. These actions will lead to new horizons. You will also eventually enjoy and treasure this new life that replaces the pain of the world of addiction. You and your families, like millions in recovery, will reap the benefits that come from overcoming incredible problems and find a new life of success that is rich in mental, emotional, physical and spiritual areas.

My approach is very personal and empathic at times and very direct at others. Both attitudes are needed as this concern is both sad yet dangerous. I find it important to be compassionate and also deliver a strong message. I want you to see how we can tackle this demanding task of getting your child and your family out from under the clutches of addiction if we work together. I know you have been lied to and undermined as parents. This type of betrayal can be somewhat consuming. I want you to know right now that I will not do that to you. A big part of my job is helping you see that I'm on your side and want the best for you. However, I cannot get your child sober and clean. You are the leverage that can. You have the bond through blood and family. You can be the reason he gets sober and clean. Let me show you how. My life's work is to help you to help your family out from the hell of this compulsion back to the joy of living. Let's do this together and "Just Say Something." Together, we'll be able to say and do a lot.

I have written Tried and True Methods to get Sober and Clean; Sober and Separated; a dissertation on Relapse Prevention for Recovering Addicts and nineteen videos on addiction under the You Tube name of The Doc Pete. I think that this is the best book I have ever published on addiction and, after pouring my heart and soul into this, my life's purpose, I'm very proud to tell you this book can save your family. It can help you to save his life. Trust my path and trust my skills, without doubt and with complete confidence, because I've helped saved hundreds of addicts and alcoholics no matter how old or what stage of addiction to which they have progressed. I have never done what I do for a living to make money and get rich. For this reason, I am not rich. I have gone bankrupt twice, trying to eke out an honest living and don't regret a minute of it. I have never had a 'mark' on my licenses for over four decades. I have slept well for many, many years and am at peace most of the time. My heart is in the right place! So is my spirit!

Recovery is not about magically being released from the spell of addiction and, therefore, I do not want to lead you down that path. Treatment will not cure your child. It will help you arrest the problem and give you time to learn about addiction. It is necessary to work at learning and practicing the directions to take in order to release your child and family from the chains of addiction that bind. There are indeed directions. The directions were written for the sole purpose of showing and motivating you, the parents, how to get this job done that has been almost impossible to do before this time. I can't do much for you unless you follow these directions. I'll explain this more in the following pages.

For the above reasons, empowerment theory (gathering strengths to control one's environment under one's own power) does not work with a 'real' addict. The ego gets in the way. The ego is that sense of overconfidence, arrogance that is present in every addict and that tells him that he is all powerful. The ego tells the addict that he can 'beat the game' and win over addiction. This thinking is followed by feelings and behaviors that eventually kill the addict. This is when intervention is necessary. Addicts need to do the opposite of fighting – they need to surrender, not be led to think they are in control and can win. We cannot beat the game. God knows we have tried! For these reasons, I have spent hours upon hours studying the different disciplines and theories to try and decipher the commonalities and develop a theory that incorporates the best and most valid and reliable 'methods' from all of the disciplines. This has been the basis for this writing. We start with the path of least resistance. Can he get sober and clean on his own (abuse)? Can he do it with individual therapy? If not, he will need more. There is family, group and combinations of these with a twelve-step program participation, outpatient groups/therapy, intensive outpatient program (IOP) and then inpatient. The point is to convince him of the need for treatment that will work.

The steps for my model overlap and seem to blend throughout. They should be done in order but sometimes it is advantageous to use parts of certain steps together. For this reason, at times I will talk about a technique used in a step before I introduce the step. My strong belief in the twelve-step direction is interwoven throughout. My belief that all of us in addictive families have been affected and need treatment is also frequently mentioned and encouraged as a direction for each of us to take. This ensures success. I am adamant about this and apologize in advance for my insistence. I insist on speaking strongly, sometimes very strongly about what I believe is right. This is life and death!

In the chapters that follow, I am going to explain addiction to you, encourage you, and show you the way out; show a way out for you, your child and your family.

Finally, I'll end by showing you the most important part - how to stay out.

Even though "96%" of alcoholics alone do not even get out of denial (Ohlms, 1996), I'll show you how to help your child do this. I know this is rather startling news, yet there may be another way to look at this startling statistic. This small percentage can motivate all when you see it as being good news for you and your child but only if you learn from this incredible statistic. Additionally, one of the more important changes you and your family will have to make is called reframing. This means that you must see this miracle of recovery as just that – a miracle instead of a curse. Also, the fact that you're interested and committed enough to find and read this book is a clear indication that you and your family are not totally trapped in the maze of denial. You and 'yours' have a good chance if you opt for treatment. You do not have to be in bondage to this disease. You do not need to be a statistic. You simply have to, like me, be "teachable." You can turn this tragedy into a miracle and thus use it to be one of the successes.

Great players want to be coached. They want to learn.
Doug Collins

CHAPTER ONE

MAKING THE DECISION - A LIFE-CHANGING MOMENT

— The only thing permanent in life is change.
Alvin Toffler

First of all, I ask you to decide whether you are the kind of parent(s) who, when your child overspends on his credit card, will pay it for him so that his credit is not harmed? Or, are you the type of parent who will let him have this learning experience so that he can correct his error and then adopt a success-oriented value system by paying his own bills and thus raising his self-esteem and sense of self-sufficiency? If you are the latter, this is the opposite of enabling or, as I call it, "accountability teaching." If you are the former, we need to talk because this is enabling. This allows him, encourages him and teaches him to invariably repeat this behavior because you have reinforced it. Now apply this reasoning to a child who is using drugs and/or alcohol. If you bail him out by paying the lawyer or the dealer, you are eliminating the consequences need for awareness of the bottom. This encourages, motivates him to continue using.

Kids do not have much of a chance to get sober and clean. Without you, it's almost impossible. I will show you the systems I have developed to ensure your success. You, as parents, are the ones who can impress upon them the harm that is being done by them to you and themselves. Analyzing, lecturing, scolding, demanding or trying to force them to stop and change their behaviors does not work. If it did, you would not be reading this book. The tactic I want you to implement consists of your sharing your pain caused by his behaviors caused by drug and/or alcohol abuse. This involves a change in the definition of the problem. The problem is not that he does not have a job. The problem is not that he has dropped out of school or is unmotivated. The problem is not that he is depressed. The problem is not that he is stealing. These are symptoms. This is the first and simplest guideline: The problem is that he has been 'consumed' with a genetic addiction that has taken over his life. We must learn how to influence him. It takes time, commitment and ongoing actions in order to arrest this treacherous disease. I will show you how to do this in the subsequent chapters.

Your Child's Mindset

As a parent, you want your child to develop character and mature into a successful adult. However, when addiction has affected him, this ability to care for self diminishes. As he uses, his judgment wanes. Then his inhibitions lower and he makes decisions that are not sound and then acts on these decisions. His brain becomes drug-impaired and he is affected by an inability to make sound judgments and practice impulse control. The frontal lobe of the brain that regulates his ability to delay gratification has been affected, not fully developed or both. He will thus have much difficulty with impulse control. This is when he will start to show signs and symptoms of addictive behavior. He will become defiant and act out of character. At this point you begin to lose your son and, in turn, begin to help him turn things around. This is your life-changing point of decision. You can either help him to get worse or help him to self-care. It is actually your decision. You are in control, only not in the usual sense. This is why it is so urgent to learn how to parent him as he progressively worsens in decision-making and his inability to effectively problem-solve. He is expecting you to take away the consequences of his addiction so that he can continue to use. This is his intent. He wants to do whatever it takes to continue to get the 'high' that is killing him. He also wants to get well. There is a part of him that cries for help. It's up to you, his parents, to help him stop by allowing him to realize that there are consequences for his using. He still thinks that he is using successfully and that it is enjoyable. The following 'types' will describe ways he may be thinking.

TABLE 1 - POTENTIAL RECOVERY MINDSETS

Cooperative –
"I've gone too far. I'll do whatever it takes, except..."

Compliant –
"I'll do this to make her (him, them) happy."

Cooperative and compliant –
"I've hurt my parents too much. I'll do whatever it takes to make it up."

Narcissistic –
"I am special, much better looking than the others, and have all of the answers."

Antisocial –
"If I don't take advantage of you, I've missed an opportunity; I've really messed up."

Omnipotent –
"I know I'm addicted but I can handle anything, it's not that bad and I intend to use again."

Overconfident – "I can always get sober again. I know."

Procrastinator - "I'll get sober tomorrow."

Defiant –
"I do whatever I want. Rules don't apply to me!"
"Yes, but..." "Don't tell me what to do."

Deceptive – "I'm going to use later, after I get them off my back because I can. I'm not really like those other people anyways."

Apathetic – "I know I'm an addict but I'm just chillin'. "I'll be fine."
"I'll do whatever it takes but I really don't know what it will take."

Teachable – "I admit, accept and approve of my disease."

All of these can get sober and clean because recovery can begin with a 'glimpse' and move forward to stable recovery if the addict has enough exposure to recovering people. The last option, teach-ability, has the best chance because he has stopped fighting and trying to do the impossible by himself.

Cooperation and teach-ability are the targeted mindsets that we want to see your child adopt. We can help him reach this point only when we heal from our hurt and anger, guilt and fear and become confident that we have a spiritual job to do with our child. When we have arrived at this point, we can then influence him to see and feel that his using is no longer getting him high.

Use these examples above to help you understand how he may think at different stages of his disease. Use them also to identify his type and therefore know how to respond to him.

You can help save his life by letting him see that he is hurting himself and others. In the following chapters I will show you specifically how to help him by not helping him.

As mentioned above, he wants help. He wants you to help. He will go in and out of denial, wanting to get clean one day and then succumbing to the cravings the next. In early recovery there seems to be a 'civil war' going on in the addict. With love and logic, we can influence him in a positive direction. He needs to be connected to others in recovery with whom he identifies. Positive peer pressure continues where we left off. We have to help him get connected to these people after we intervene. This ensures good recovery. Without this, he may not have a chance!

He needs you, as parents, to help him. My goal is to show you how to do this effectively. This you can do at once by holding him accountable for his dysfunctional behaviors that are consequences of his using. Connect the problems to his drug and/or alcohol use as he cannot yet see this. This will, in turn, eventually empower him.

An example of teaching a child to learn accountability and not enabling happened to me when I was a child. When I was twelve years old, I fell in love with and wanted this red Schwin bicycle with double crossbars from the handlebars to the seat with thin tires and such a sleek look that I had to have it. I asked my father if I could get it and he told me to get a job. I knew that this decision was non-negotiable. It was a message given to me that 'shaped' my belief in earning my own way yet, more importantly, my belief in myself that "I could do it." I also knew that when my father said something, he meant it. I experienced one of those life-changing moments that I have benefited from for decades. I have never once doubted my ability to take care of myself. It's one of my father's greatest gifts to me. As a result, I started mowing lawns all around the neighborhood for twenty-five cents a lawn (this was in 1957), got a paper route, shoveled snow in the winter and saved up the money over time. I'll never forget the jobs because I got the feeling of self-sufficiency at age twelve. What a time it was! Mickey Mantle was in a zone and Joe Dimaggio was 'King of the Road'; Elvis was singing "Blue Suede Shoes," the Beatles were on their way and we hadn't even heard of Larry Bird or Michael Jordon yet. This feeling of achievement was icing on the cake. I got the bike.

Because of this, I had a canary yellow convertible 1967 Jaguar XKE, a Master's degree in counseling and was supervising a suicide hotline of a mental health center by twenty-four years of age. I got there by going to school full time at night while teaching, commuting 40 miles each way on icy roads on a daily basis. I really didn't think this was a big deal because I had been programmed to work and earn my way. I had a work ethic and not a sense of entitlement. You see, my father and mother had been through the depression in America in the 20's and knew the value of good habits and earning my way. My father believed in the American Dream and went from poverty to a family with seven children, coped with the tragic death of his wife in his 20's and remarried and never divorced. He became the president of Syracuse Engineering in his 30's after his boss told him that he was not smart enough to become a Professional Engineer (PE). As a result, he modeled the "American Dream" for me. I was happy to have a job and felt fortunate to have the opportunity to work and earn my way.

So, you see I learned how to take care of myself and had the attitude that, "I was responsible for myself and was also capable." What I never had, never once thought, never ever believed was that, "the world owes me a living." In fact, the opposite attitude is necessary to get sober and clean. This is one of the reasons why I've been sober and clean for over twenty-five years without a relapse. Only you can give this attitude to your child just like my father did for me. It's never too late to do this!

My mother is kind and wise and gentle and intelligent. Having been close to God for her entire life, she has many of the character assets that we have to develop in order to stay sober. I was able to recognize how to get humble and open-minded and willing to change because I had seen her exemplify this all throughout my life. When I had to become these things in order to save my life, I could use the modeling of these attributes that she taught me when I was growing up. These came somewhat easy to me as they were familiar. I owe her my recovery. She taught me gratitude before I knew what it was.

I have seen the opposite - an attitude of entitlement - as an impediment, a recipe for relapse, for many of the thousands I have seen try to get sober even when they desperately want to get sober and clean. The discipline is simply not there, not that getting sober and clean is merely a matter of discipline. However, it does take an attitude of accountability. You can teach this to him at any age. The point I'm trying to teach is that, the sooner you begin to teach accountability, the better chance your child will have to survive this deadly brain disease of addiction. I have studied this process for almost 50 years and have it 'down' very well. I have learned the process to a T. Let me show you how to be one of the successes. One of the most important lessons involves using a caring attitude yet sending a message that you mean business. As stated before, you don't want to be too stern as this will sabotage the intervention!!!

96% of alcoholics do not get out of denial (Ohms, 1991). This is an incredible statistic. We don't want your child to be in the 4% bracket. We want him in the top 2%! This sounds like a better idea, doesn't it? I will use my education at the Ph.D. level, years of experience working with addicts and alcoholics, my experience of having directed and owned two treatment centers and still operating one and consulting with others to teach you how to be successful. In addition, my dedication to keeping up with the latest information, my own Tried and True system, theories and techniques in the addictions field, my open-mindedness and ability to bond and cooperate with you and your family will help you to save your child. Together, we can do this. I can help you with this. I want to do this!

Eyes are more accurate witnesses than ears. Heraclitus c. 540 - c. 480 BC

CHAPTER TWO

WHAT IS ADDICTION?

Addiction is the pursuit of happiness in the absence of pleasure.
R. Heilman

The Disease Concept

When the family can understand this disease and see their part in it, they can begin to heal. Up to this point, they are stuck in a maze of confusion, hurt, guilt, fear, frustration and shame. Other attempts to see this problem as something else leads to failure. This is inevitable, given the nature of this problem. No one wants it in the family, few will talk about it and all will want it gone while not knowing what it is. However, reality is that it has been and is in your family. Let's work together to arrest it.

Many people have written about the disease concept of alcoholism. The literature is still mixed and conflicting. After studying this problem for decades, my belief is that addicts have addictive thoughts, cravings, and loss of control and relapse behaviors that normal people do not have. This may offend an otherwise normal person's sense of pride as it taps into the stigmas of addiction. Most people still think that it's a matter of intent, will power. This is because most people, probably nine out of ten, did stop abusing alcohol after the first bad experience. They never got the cravings nor did they have a pre-genetic disposition that created these cravings. The addict knows this and must create a solid and rigid mindset that leads him to believe that he is also a normal drinker or drug user. This way he avoids the shame of addiction and can continue to use.

However, we have to see that we also have been affected by this misinformation and have learned to judge the addict due to this stigma associated with the problem. This stigma is wrong. Think of addiction as a disease, similar to diabetes. We don't judge diabetics and insist that they make insulin and stop the stupid behavior. We need to have the same attitude about addiction. In fact, addiction is much worse than other diseases because it takes away not only health but also everything else. Think about it. It takes away relationships, love, careers, children, parents, mental and emotional health, freedom, minds, and whatever else the addict has. Do you really think anyone chooses this? We must see this side of addiction if we are to be the healers. Yes, this is what we have to be. I'm asking you to 'rise to this occasion' and help your child heal when no one else can.

I believe in "holistic treatment," and have since the 1980's, focusing not only on abstinence, but also on the spiritual side of the addict/alcoholic, the mind, emotional life and body. However, there is an unordered order to recovery. First has to be the spiritual conversion. Then the timing comes into play. This has to be a strong consideration. Some people get sober and quit cigarettes immediately. Some wait a year or so. Some get their jobs back soon, some their teeth. Some repair the relationships quickly. Some don't. We don't really know when changes take place because, in recovery, most things unfold as we develop spiritually. This is difficult to explain but I do know that, when in good quality recovery, we have a chance to develop in every area of life. The important concern is to encourage the addict in the depleted areas but not force change that will induce stress and relapse.

Bring your dreams to the Program.
Bill Oakley

There is a chance for all other areas of life to become more functional if the addict/alcoholic abstains and develops spiritually, both coinciding. I have worked with many parents who fought and fought for months when we had helped the child to get 6 or seven months of recovery, attend meetings, get a sponsor, work the twelve steps and be far ahead of others, far ahead of the norm, yet parents had very high standards for them that actually sabotaged their recovery. Jobs needed to be obtained, rooms needed to be cleaned and relationships needed to be repaired. The old anger and fears must dissipate or parents will 'act out' on these feelings, have a rigid need to control and demand much more than the child can do. Al-Anon helps incredibly with patience and tolerance as well as expectations. Treatment can help your child to regulate recovery tasks so that home life is more manageable. I strongly agree that goals for recovery definitely include job, work, better relationship, structure, hygiene, health and all of the 'normal' desires that parents want for their child. The 'key' is to prioritize meetings and steps and sponsorship so that your child can, as a result of doing these things, become healthy enough to develop spiritually (first) and then mentally, physically and emotionally. The order and timing are paramount. When working the steps in a twelve-step Program, I have been amazed at how the 'issues' such as shame, relationship enhancement, self-esteem, accountability, amends, resentment, self-deception, thievery, self-centeredness, fear and inconsideration have been addressed as the person worked their Program. If I had to focus on too many of these at once or even issues that others wanted me to focus on, I would have been drunk and high within the first month. In early recovery, real change, Real Recovery occurs only if we see that it is necessary and will benefit us. The good news is that we can get him there.

This disease is not very well understood but is highly treatable. However, it is important not to call it something else because it makes it easier to accept. If you have cancer, you do not call it a heat rash. If you call it something else other than cancer, you will treat something else other than the cancer. You will not treat the cancer. You won't be able to until you find out what you have. This problem needs to be arrested also. When an addict/alcoholic is active in his or her addiction, in other words using, the others problems/behaviors do not get treated. The aberrant behavior remains because the addict/alcoholic still behaves like an active addict. There is no 'recovery motivation' to change behaviors. Even if the person is abstinent but not in recovery, he may be worse off than when using. He has no relief from the pain and is still creating problems.

Euphoria

I have learned that about one in ten Americans has the disease of alcoholism. The rate of addiction in general is more likely one in eight. When this person drinks alcohol or uses drugs, there is a feeling which is euphoric. This may come at first use of the drug or later after an unspecified period of time. Normal people do not get this feeling nor do they chase this feeling for years without getting it. They do not get cravings either. They can stop. An addict cannot without a spiritual conversion. This is what I believe.

Progression

Further, when the addict/alcoholic uses, the problem eventually becomes overwhelming. In early stages, the problem sometimes can be arrested easily (yet it is usually not). After an adaptation period of several weeks to several years (depending on the individual person), quitting becomes almost impossible. The problem follows a path, has symptoms and, like most diseases, has a cause which is difficult to determine. It is treatable but is very elusive. As the person drinks or drugs more and more, the cravings begin to develop and tolerance builds. Then there are problems such as shame, fear, unpredictability, social ineptness and so on. Normal drinkers or persons would quit when there is a problem because they have been doing it perhaps as a "phase" similar to what college students or younger non addicts sometimes do. They can see the problems and do not put up with the pain. An alcoholic/addict will put up with the pain and does not quit. The addict cannot easily quit. Many researchers say addicts cannot quit at all. The point is that they are not drinking or abusing drugs to harm anyone. It 'comes with the territory'. It comes with the addiction. It is not personal, even when the addict takes out his or her pain on another person. Without the substance and when in recovery, most addicts are decent human beings. There is a small percentage who are sociopaths or mentally ill. However, I believe this is a very small percentage.

What you also need to know is that the disease seems to have a life of its own. By this I mean that the user has to develop a way to think, to rationalize, to deny, to intellectualize and to blame others in order to continue. In order to continue his use, the addict/alcoholic has to develop characteristics and behaviors that he would not ordinarily have for any other reason. He or she has to protect the mind from the truth that the problem is harming others and killing him/her. When you cannot stop and have to have the 'change in feeling' so badly that you will lie and cheat and steal and blame and criticize and let the rage and fears devour you, the problem is extreme and has progressed to an end-stage. It now has a life of its own. It has progressively become worse.

In addition, it never gets better. If it did, addicts/alcoholics could 'cut back' or control it. The abstinence theory makes sense to me for this and the above reasons. The true addict/alcoholic cannot return to social drinking or use of drugs. I have seen many people attempt to beat the game and die trying. I have been open-minded over the years and have read and studied the different theories and approaches and have actually looked for other ways to treat this problem. I have been convinced that the disease concept is the only one that makes sense. We can't 'buy into' different approaches touted by "theorists" who have not been there, have studied the problem only in school or have not read or used valid and reliable research to establish their treatment theories. The problem, your child, is too important to take 'lightly' and treat other than with methods that really work.

This problem develops until it kills the user and greatly harms the people surrounding the user. Yes, there is a point of no return for many addicts/alcoholics who risk their lives daily. Some give up and, even if they have been sober before, stop trying to get sober again, regardless of consequences. However, there is a way to combat the problem. It is called Surrender to Win. It involves a 'cease fire' for good. The addict can do this, pray, detach from the problem by going to AA or NA and/or by learning the 'path' taught there or both. There are probably groups in your city or town.

Co-addiction

Codependency is when a person's job is to fix another person but they really don't want them fixed because then they'll be out of work. Bill Riedler

The emotional damage done to the people surrounding the addict is immense. The damage also occurs physically, spiritually, and mentally. The problems that stem from these are many. For different reasons, the co-addict has a need to remain with the addict. Unintentionally, this person supports the addiction, enabling the addict to continue their addiction. The relationship with the addict/alcoholic is usually nonthreatening, at times even one which complies with the addict's behavior. The enabler becomes obsessed with the addict and even 'addicted' to the person. He has to comply with the addiction or the addict rebels and fights the co-addict. Co-addicts usually hate controversy. Through this process, the addiction stays alive.

Further, the addict has to take the focus away from the disease or denial is threatened and in danger of being broken. As above, some co-addicts unknowingly go along with the behavior up to a point or to the end. As the disease becomes apparent they may detach. Others stay until the disease consumes them also. To the addict, the substance is so seductive and "needed" that anything or anybody who threatens the denial will be attacked. If you feel attacked, this is why. Don't buy into the blame, judgments, yelling, criticizing. This is not your fault!

Lastly, no one person causes it. My belief is that the disease of addiction is mostly a matter of genetics. The disease progressively gets worse. It never gets better. It is not acute. That is, it does not get cured like a broken arm. It is lasting, never going away. Most importantly, it can be arrested with a spiritual conversion, found through AA or NA. Al-Anon works for the co-addict. Please go to learn this path of recovery.

Remember, it's not your fault!

The family disease of addiction

Notice that I said family. One of the most important lessons is that this is a family illness and the family needs treatment. You may object to this at first as you seem to have been the stable ones, the ones trying to help. In the past, I thought this also. After all, I'm the helper, not the patient. However, when I became enmeshed enough with trying to help someone who did not want help as much as I wanted it for him, and in enough emotional pain from anger, hurt, guilt and fear, I could then see how I was a part of the problem. It was difficult to be present, in the moment. My thought process would focus on useless rumination about the person I was trying to help. Fear would drive me to tomorrow and frustration to yesterday. I prefer to be in today as this is where life is going on. Through treatment, I have learned that I have to take care of myself first as I cannot help anyone if I'm other-focused. This has been painful but I believe the only choice. When I entered treatment for my addiction to an addict, I could then free myself from enabling, doing for others what they can and should do for themselves, by helping only those who wanted help. I urge you to try this approach. Then you can enjoy life at a greater level and be a great role model for your son.

Your self-care actually builds your credibility with him and can actually help him to recover. However, if you're pre-occupied with him, he will know it and feel this protection and he won't have to take any action. He will know that you are there for him always and will bail him out always. This will keep him stuck! Let's become part of the solution.

Your child may not want help now but we'll do all we can to get him to a place where he does. Then we can stand by his side and help by supporting his recovery. However, if we try to force him to get help when he doesn't want help, it may backfire. This is co-dependency. We're the ones who are then hurting the most. We have to then decide if we are willing to let this problem of addiction consume us also, even though it does so in a different manner. It does so by leading us to an emotionally distraught, angry and helpless place. Let's get you out before that happens. When we let go, he can then enter treatment (Al-Anon teaches this). Even better, let's 'strike while the iron is hot', when he has a chance to get out of denial and 'come around' to embrace recovery. Then we have done our part to help him to recovery.

Family Team

The family is still the cornerstone of society and always has been. A strong family can accomplish anything. The fact that you are reading this book suggests that you still have hope in your family. You are still committed to healing your family and that means that there is great hope.

Addiction affects everyone in the family on an emotional, mental, social and physical level, not to mention spiritual. It creates walls that we must tear down. Forming and remaining a strong team as a family is the best chance all and any of the family members have to detach from the consequences of this treacherous disease. Your job, no matter what your role is in the family, your job is to stay healthy and learn as much as you can about addiction from reliable sources. In my opinion, the most reliable sources are those who have successfully succeeded in doing just that, overcoming addiction and then prospering. Learn from those who have been there. Otherwise, you will get the wrong information. You could very well end up working on the wrong problem and thus the wrong solution. Without help, this is what happens!

Splitting

In an addictive family, splitting is a term used to describe the division of a team in an attempt to foster disunity and therefore bring one of the parties to the side of the addict. Splitting can occur on a sports team, a debating team, in government, in a school, a church and almost any organization or institution. Imagine addiction as being an entity that splits the family members to include parents, siblings and extended members. There is a divisive effect on all. The disease will coax all to take sides against each other, never knowing what normal is, defending the addict and then the victims. Remember, it has a life of its own. It can get very confusing and chaotic.

On the other hand, I want to reassure the entire family of the success to come if you remain united against the addiction. You have started off in the right direction with the right resource – me or someone like me. Treatment is very successful when you enlist the help of an expert to keep you focused on recovery and you have come to the right place. As a result, you will not split the family. You can work toward mending relationships, uniting against the disease, not against each other. You will find great strength in numbers.

The Real Problem

This book was written in the year 2011 and it is based on over 45 years of my dedicated work and study. I have spent nearly a half of a century learning and studying addiction from a personal, professional and concerned perspective. I have been mostly influenced by the disease concept of addiction, self-help, mental health training and the blending of marriage and family counseling in which I have been licensed since 1981. I have become convinced that the problem is not a moral dilemma, does not stem from a psychological cause and that abstinence is required if a person is truly an addict. Feelings do not cause addiction. Parenting does not cause addiction. Environment does not cause addiction. These factors may contribute to whether a person begins but do not contribute to an addict's ability to stop. A non-addict who has been poorly parented, coming from a broken home, having a physical handicap, having a mental illness, brought up in the worst section of town, with low self-esteem and poor intelligence will quit using drugs and/or alcohol if it causes problems that he connects to the ingestion!

Genetics cause addiction. Some genetic factor interferes with the addict's ability to stop the self-destruction. I do believe that after the addict crosses into middle stages, most if not all moral, psychological, social, emotional and environmental problems are always caused by the disease. These must be addressed in recovery. However, these are always results of drug and alcohol addiction. Let's not get confused with cause and effect!

Commitment

Together we can detach from this hopeless state back to hope and sanity. Treatment works. Addiction treatment is very successful when sought sincerely and when the family is willing to do 'whatever it takes.' I have found a way to help the family and, therefore, your child out from this hellhole. I can help you to get your child to listen to you so that you can motivate him. Treatment breeds success but only under certain conditions. I can and will teach you these conditions.

You have to be committed all the way. You cannot let your guard down. Even when he is in recovery, in the maintenance stage, he can become complacent. He may stop attending his meetings and praying and/or go back to sleeping late or any of the behaviors that he was doing when he was using. In other words, he will regress. Hopefully, you will know that you cannot 'buy into this complacency' and watch him go backwards, hoping that he will be fine. He may tell you he is fine but you hopefully will know enough to 'trust his actions' and not what he says. More on this to come in later pages.

The Goal

The goal is to bring your child 'to decision' so that he can make the commitment to do whatever it takes to abstain. Success can occur when enablers cease to enable and the addict then feels the pain and loss or anticipation of the problems; then and only then can recovery occur. This cannot be forced. It has to be a result of influence. The addict has a defiance, overt and/or covert, that is equal to none. It can't be forced by the government, the judge, the dope dealers or lecturers. In fact, these entities can have the opposite effect on the addict. They can trigger the defiance the addict has for rules and even 'fix' the denial. Recovery has to be initiated by the addict after an honest self-diagnosis by him. The best vehicle to accomplish this miracle is within the context of the family when enablers change and hold the addict accountable. This can motivate him. He may then be able to realize that it's in his best interests to stop. It starts and ends with the family.

Relapse

It is impossible to live without failing at something, unless you live so cautiously that you might as well not have lived at all. J.K. Rowling

Certain truths need to be adopted by the family and then actions based upon these beliefs need to be practiced on a continual basis in order to begin recovery and thus motivate the addict, help him to recover and stay recovered. Two basic truths form the basis for this book. One is from the studies of W. Penfield who spoke of the family as being the child's first classroom. If this is true, then this leads to the second truth that the parents are the child's first teachers.

Penfield's (1951) studies also suggested that memory is constant and timeless and, although unconscious at times, retrievable if triggered. Depok Chopra (1991) also reported that, 'the memory of the euphoric feeling never goes away.' This gives great insight into our study on addiction as it gives an explanation for relapse. The addict enjoys the substance, and then later puts up with it because of rewards from the pleasure centers of the brain as well as the presence of cravings. In addition, he develops a way to justify using the drug after it causes problems. The memory of the pleasure, even if not recent, persists. This thinking persists even when he is abstinent. Both the reminders and the thinking have to be treated after the detoxification from the drug is begun. The addict will remember the pleasure of the early euphoria forever. He will not remember the pain unless he is reminded frequently. In addition to reading theory on addictive memory and experiencing it, I have heard about this phenomenon from hundreds of addicts/alcoholics. In spite of intense pain and loss, the addict remembers only the once-felt pleasure, the good times. This is called euphoric recall. It is based on warped thinking. However, this can be treated. Ongoing twelve-step meetings will remind the addict if he attends them.

The Learning that Enables

It follows that the addict and the family have to change the majority of their thinking about this problem. The family can help to create this needed foundation. Much of the change for the addict and the family members involves a paradigm shift, a shift in thinking. Thoughts that tend to minimize or justify the problems caused by the abuse of drugs and/or alcohol have to be changed. Reality-based thinking must be learned and integrated. In addition, the feelings and behaviors have to change. This entails major work on self and less work on others. In fact, it takes no work on others. This takes much time to master. It takes much effort toward studying the problem intensely and not trying to 'fix' others. It takes the courage to begin work on our pain.

In order to be motivated for this change the family must want it desperately as a result of connecting their problems as well as the child's problems to the addiction and seeing the downward spiral as always getting worse, never better, and ending in death. This downward spiral ends in death of all either physically, psychologically, socially and/or spiritually. You MUST stop protecting the abuser from the consequences needed for motivation to get sober or no one gets better. Then change becomes possible. Then our children can prosper. Only when friends and family stop shielding the person from the pain is recovery possible. Remember, he is addicted to drugs and/or alcohol. Don't become addicted to him.

This is most easily seen when observing some celebrities trying to survive addiction. They are coddled and protected by mostly everyone in their business for reasons mostly a-spiritual. They will not get help because they usually have enablers – people who shield them from the pain and loss needed in order to recover. These may be agents, teachers, siblings, grandparents, spouses, girlfriends, dealers, bartenders, colleagues, coaches, or anyone who puts up with his lies and cheating and whatever aberrant behaviors.

In order to succeed, we must heed the advice and experiences of those who have survived and learned to prosper. There are people who have overcome these enabling behaviors. They are the experts. They can guide you. The disease is easy to see and work with when you want guidance, have sought it and have it. We can stand on the shoulders of those who have found the solution.

The Main Obstacle

Addiction has many ways to harm and must be 'countered' with strong and consistent actions. However, there is a major obstacle that sabotages recovery success. The number one reason for treatment failure involves fear of change (adherence to the status quo), a change of mind, a change of values, a change of character, a change from the damage done to self and a change of focus to others. This transformation needs to happen and if it does not, it is then and only then that the addict and the co-addict err and fall prey to this problem. The new thinking that is necessary for 'recovery entry' can seem very illogical because it is not acceptable thinking in most areas of life. Surrendering is never very palatable until you, the parents, understand the downward spiral of addiction and the upward process of recovery. It is such a new mindset that few families affected by addiction will adopt it until they have exhausted all other avenues. It is one of many recovery paradoxes.

All family members must become teachable. This does not come easily to the family members. The problem actually centers on the concept that the student wants to be the teacher. The change involves changing the belief that you have to control and fix the problem because that is your job as a parent. Your child has been consumed by an addiction, is lost and this happened under your roof. This shock eventually wears off and, if you enter treatment and become educated with accurate information, you can recover. You have to become the student.

This is the number one rule for the family members: Be the student!

Parents, addict, siblings, other relatives and all else involved should follow treatment steps that have been tried, tested and proven to be effective. This begins with early recovery and involves open-mindedness. Rigid thinking must be replaced with flexible thinking. We in recovery should be rigid about abstinence from all mood-altering chemicals to include alcohol but flexible about everything else. We must be ready to change our minds tomorrow on anything we think today except our ideas regarding abstinence.

If I came to your business to work, I would ask you to direct me. However, with addiction, there is some phenomenon that makes us want to do it our way. If that worked you would have solved the problem already. You would not have an unsolved problem. In fact, I would suspect that you have tried many ways to arrest this problem. We, as co-addicts, are like the addict who tries time and again to get sober and clean by himself. He exerts much effort and eventually gives up and gives in. We can't let this happen to us or our children. With a unified effort, we can arrest this. It takes a leader who has studied this deadly problem and knows how to address it, coach the family to recovery and help the addict enter treatment. Find such a therapist and let him lead. Give the therapist permission to be the therapist and coach you to lead your family through this maze.

I advise parents and their child and other family members to read and study this book in its entirety. The problem of addiction has many ways to harm us and must be 'reversed' via accurate thinking and strong actions. Learning the way to recovery by assimilating accurate information and taking actions based on this information is imperative. Over and over, I have and will remind you to recover according to directions. This disease is not your typical problem that can be solved with a strong will, moving, substituting new behaviors, getting a new job or giving up a relationship. This change involves a spiritual change, an evolution, a transformation. In order to achieve this, we need a spiritual guide. We have to be the student. We must be teachable. This is the best way to proceed is as a student. Most leaders have advisors. Let me do what I do best – teach. I will teach you practical, step-by-step, systematic, time-tested and true methods that are in simple language and aimed at arresting this horrendous disease.

My directions work. I have studied hard and long, had many successes and can lead you out of this hell. My only request is that you ask me questions, ask others about me, read my testimonials on my websites, read my writings, watch me work and then trust me and do as I suggest and as I do. I do these things that I say work. I am very 'seasoned' with this concern and haven't had a drug or drink since 1986. I trust God and try to help people who ask for help. I've made it "right" with the people I've harmed. I live in peace and inspiration. I have done that which I ask you and your child to do. Let me show you how to do this. I can show you and your child how to rise from the depths of addiction to peace of mind and sound living.

One More Time - Relapse Thoughts.

A few years ago, I worked with a 40 year old man who started with alcohol and pot and whatever other drugs were around in his high school. He had some concerns, i.e., hangovers, a bad relationship, overspending and decided to quit drinking so much, slow down and control his problem (addiction). He was able to do this somewhat for a while during his twenty's, always returning to his addiction even after months of abstinence. As a result of this, he formed a thought process that stated that he could control his use whenever he chose (through his will power) and held on to that belief system until he was knee-deep in his addiction. Even in his thirties, when he began to progress to opiates, benzodiazepines and whatever he could get when he had nothing, he hung onto the idea that he could control his addiction. Even when he was sober a year and one half and relapsed, he held on to the old idea that he could control his use.

What is typical for the addict, yet difficult for others to see is that there is a rigid thought process that tells the person that he can try using one more time. This consists of many thoughts that all lead to ways of justifying an addiction. When an addict cannot quit, he already has developed an iron clad thought process that consists of many beliefs, all having the purpose of continued use.

TABLE 2 – THE ADDICT'S RELAPSE THOUGHTS

Addictive thought processes can take many forms. Below are the main 'arguments' and are usually summed up in several different yet connected basic beliefs. These beliefs, not reality-based, are comprised of the notion that he can control his addiction. This has lead to the demise of many, probably most, addicts/alcoholics. The responses that I want you to practice are also similar in nature and can be personalized to fit your communication style. Reality-based responses have a core belief such as: "I love you and I want you to rethink what you are saying." A "loved one" can help him see things differently if the relationship is intact, i.e., caring and trusting. It also is significant if he has made the connection between using and problems. He will then be able to recall the irrational thinking when reminded. Responses need to be caring and firm, reality-based with a caring and assertive tone. A "broken record" technique is very powerful and involves repetition of your message without getting sidetracked. By doing this, you can be very consistent. The relapse thoughts are followed by possible responses (R. = response) and are as follows:

Table 2 - Relapse Beliefs

"I can stop tomorrow."

R. "Then wait until tomorrow to start." or
"You told us you couldn't control it anymore." or
"Any attempt will fail."

"I can certainly do this one more time."

R. "Why would you want to?" or
"You've run out of ways to control your addiction."

"This time I can handle it."

R. "You've never been able to before."

"I'll just have one."

R. "When was the last time you had just one?" or
"Listen, God gave you a daily reprieve. Don't sabotage Him."

"I now understand addiction now so I can do it again."

R. "Knowledge doesn't stop the cravings or compulsion." or
"Any attempt will fail."

"I haven't drunk in over a year so I'm sure I can drink safely now."

R. "Why would you want to ruin a good thing?" or "Any attempt will fail."

"I have a year clean and sober so I'm going to celebrate." or "No one will know."

R. "What happened the last time you used?" or
"Celebrate your recovery, not your relapse." or "You'll know."

"I have twenty years clean and sober so maybe I'm not a real alcoholic and can drink."

R. "You know it gets progressively worse!" or
"Remember, you told me you were a real alcoholic."

"I can surely smoke pot or have a beer because I haven't used oxycontin for two years."

R. "You know better than that; it will lead back to opiates!" or
"You know that there's a relapse you don't come back from."

"I kicked heroin so alcohol is really no problem."

R. "Why go back?" or "You know you're fooling yourself." or
"You know this is bad thinking."

"I can run five miles and, therefore, I'm ok."

R. "Did you work out when you were high or drunk?" or
"There's no connection between the two."

"I'm working and am very functional."

R. "You were before also." or "Your recovery is working and that's the reason you're doing well." or "Don't let what you got back take you back."

Learn some of these responses so that your communication, your response, can be spontaneous. You don't want to appear unconfident or confused. He needs you to help him think. His brain has been altered.

This model of responses is very personal to me. When I was about six weeks sober and clean I had the idea that I would go to Daytona Beach for my yearly "mental health weekend." My buddy, Scott, who knew recovery like the "back of his hand" simply asked me, "Did you ever go to Daytona and not get high?" That got me to think about my last trip there which was a complete nightmare. I didn't go. I trusted him very much and I knew that he knew addiction backwards and forwards. You see, his mother married seven alcoholics so he therefore knew addiction "up close and personal."

More Obvious and Blatant Relapse Thoughts are more direct. "Leave me alone," is an example. At this point, the addict is not even concerned about others. He does not care about the pain inflicted on "loved ones."

Other relapse thoughts, Deceptive and Self-deceptive Beliefs are also characterized by overconfidence. These statements are warning signs that your child is again thinking that he is 'in charge,' that he knows what he is doing. They are usually followed by complacency, a mindset that indicates that he will soon and probably already have discontinued the behaviors (meetings, sponsorship, prayer…) that got him sober and clean. By this time you probably have learned that Real Recovery consists of adopting a lifestyle with a daily program that is continual throughout one's life. So perhaps you can recognize some of these thoughts. Examples of these are:

"I'll never drink or drug again." Addicts who think this usually relapse.

"I'll do whatever it takes." However, when asked to attend '90 & 90' or go inpatient or anything they don't want to do, they refuse.

"I'm fine." or "I'm ok now."
This usually means lack of any insights or awareness of feelings.

"I can do this." He is not at all aware of his many attempts at recovery.

These thoughts are difficult for the parent to 'read' at times because they do sound positive. However, once you can understand the addictive mind, you can see through these thoughts. It is more difficult for the loving and hopeful parent to 'see through' these statements because these are the thoughts you have been waiting to hear. They are so much different than before. However, they are still based on denial, a different type of denial. I call this controlled denial as opposed to the full-blown denial that characterized his complete inability to admit to the problem in spite of serious consequences.

Another set of beliefs are recovery beliefs. These are based on recovery goals and actions, are positive statements and suggest that he is in Real Recovery. The following are examples of this thinking:

"God is good."

"I'm sorry."

"I really messed things up."

"Can I get you anything from the store?"

"I need a meeting."

"I may be wrong but…"

"Sorry about being late."

"I need a meeting."

"I need to call my sponsor."

"Can I have a ride to a meeting?"

Self-Efficacy

In good recovery, these insane beliefs must be replaced over the years with reality-based thoughts. In good recovery they are replaced. This begins to happen during step two of the twelve-step programs. Thinking becomes flexible; the addict/alcoholic is able to think positively. In fact, the person who was severely handicapped with powerlessness over his addiction can progress to a recovery level whereas he is performing daily tasks that protect him from the temptations of the addiction. He is avoiding temptations, praying, talking to recovering people, learning how to think recovery thoughts, reading recovery literature daily and is in a 'safe' zone as long as he continues this daily pattern. The feeling of confidence, not over-confidence, as a result of practicing this lifestyle is called self-efficacy.

A normal person could see the insanity. An addict cannot. This is called self-deception. This self-talk is subconscious. However, as stated before, the truth becomes available only when problems emerge and the addict can feel the pain and loss and thus become motivated. We cannot talk them or coerce them out of the insanity. The addict must self-diagnose based on the pain resulting from the problems caused by the drinking or drug use. If we provide a solution to the problem, he will not have to do this for himself. He may not be able to do so.

The above client came back after the relapse and we mutually discover two flaws in his previous attempt at recovery. These were based on the thinking that he did not have to do these things like others did. He was better than them. One flaw was that he was not connected to a Higher Power and the other was that he was not connected to his twelve-step Program. He was going to meetings but not really committed. He began to pray, go to meetings early, leave late, and looked for someone to help. In other words, he began to sincerely practice spiritual principles that were tailored to recovery tasks that work. From that point he stayed sober and clean and probably will as long as he keeps doing these things plus more. After all, why would an addict stop doing what works? As long as we attend our program, we have an opportunity to stay sober because we stay sane in knowing that "Any attempt at drinking or drugging will be the end of me."

The above describes the direction your son has taken and also the direction he must take in order to reverse the addiction. In Young Recovery, my intensive outpatient treatment program for young adults, we teach the three 'r's': RRR. This stands for Relapse Risk Reduction and is a technique of systematic desensitization that places the addict in the 'real world' where they become exposed to relapse triggers and new experiences and then feel uncomfortable. They then can process the fears and resentments, guilt and hurt that they may feel when in the mainstream of life. Outpatient treatment is a good vehicle for getting used to the 'real world' due to the reality that they are not in a laboratory setting and are exposed daily to the relapse triggers. This can make the difference between success and failure. We don't protect them from this exposure but get them to cope with these triggers. We also help them to remove the using friends from their lives. This is the number one relapse trigger that they must give up. I will show you that which I know is true and that works. I pray you follow my lead. The directions unfold as follows. Let's begin!

CHAPTER THREE

A FURTHER LOOK INSIDE THE MIND OF AN ADDICT/ALCOHOLIC CHILD AND HOW TO HELP

An addict's mind is like a bad neighborhood.
Its' owner should never go there alone.
Anonymous

In the pages that follow, which I want you to read and study carefully, I'm going to share my 45 plus years of experience in the field of addictions, give you accurate information about this problem, empathize (not sympathize) with your predicament, tell about my journey from hell to heaven and show you how to save your child. Throughout this book, I will explain the intricacies of addiction to include addictive thinking, feeling and behavior, especially as it pertains to untreated addiction. As a result, you will hopefully be able to see the problem as a sickness and not react negatively to the negative behavior but act rationally and assertively. We cannot avoid judging and being offended by this problem until we can see it as the illness that it is. The American Society of Addiction Medicine now defines the problem as a brain disorder of reward that a profound effect on brain circuitry AND is characterized by loss of control has. This means that it is a genetic disease that affects the brain that involves heredity and loss of freedom to choose. Thinking is impaired and unrealistic, formed solely to justify self-destruction that leads to annihilation. Addicts do not choose this path. They inherit it. To get sober and clean this thinking must change from justifying to accepting recovery. When we understand this, we can then use our reasoning and not take the behavior personally. We can think rationally.

Using this new mindset you, as parents, can be effective and therefore get the results that you want. It is then that your responses will be the ones that you want to use. You'll talk to your child the way that you choose, thus gaining his respect while 'getting through' to him at the same time. You can practice thinking about this problem differently so that you can keep yourself from reacting.

What can I say to prepare you as parents and family for this journey from the downward addiction progression to the upward progression of recovery that awaits you? How can I build the trust necessary for recovery from the betrayal and dark experiences you've had with this treacherous problem? These are things I have often asked myself. My journey as a therapist trying to arrest this dilemma has been long and hard, filled with pain, joy, success, relapse and heartache, both mine and others. I have had to reevaluate my techniques, theory, skills and delivery since 1965 when I first encountered this problem. I am still learning and the road can be discouraging but I never give up. I stay teachable and spiritual. Pride is the enemy. Prayer and recovery actions are the solution. Let's study your child's personal journey into addiction so that we can walk him out to recovery.

You probably are discouraged, perhaps even somewhat hopeless. When I get discouraged, I oftentimes have to remind myself of the successes and the positive feedback I have received over the years. I know that this disease can convince us that things are hopeless but there is hope. We give it to each other. In the addiction counseling arena, there exists much burnout. In the family, it's called chaos, panic and crisis. I know full well how this feels. I know the hurt and the rage and the manipulations and mistrust and the fears from both sides, from my former active addiction and treating active addiction. I've been both places. I also know how to cope with this and function in an effective, healthy manner. This qualifies me to guide you out of the addiction hell into recovery – the journey back to a normal, peaceful, reality-based life with its regularity and love and holidays and celebrations and so forth. I know how to overcome the pain and return to a life worth celebrating. I have done this and given it to hundreds since my return. I can and will do this for you also. You simply have to give me permission to be the therapist.

My experience, education and recovery qualify me to lead families from this predicament. Trust me, there is hope! I see it daily. I can show you if you let me. Again, you must first give me permission to be the therapist, the coach, the guide. My approach requires that you let me place you in charge and also let me help you with mutual goals and house rules as well as ongoing decision-making, boundary setting and adjustment to relapse triggers and subsequent cravings. In other words, we have to learn to respect each others' opinions and beliefs and work together. We have to let go of the tendency to control each other and also your child. You have to rely on me the same way your child must rely on you. You'll see that I repeat myself often because the change in thinking that is required to respond effectively to this disease bears repetition. Therefore, I repeat myself often and intentionally as I explain the journey into addiction and the path from the pain.

CHAPTER FOUR

PERSONAL HISTORY

I was a high bottom drunk until God restored my memory.
Doc Pete

In 1965, I took a family course at Niagara University. I learned that family is the most important force in a person's life. Then I spent over forty-five years working with families. I have been influenced by and learned much from those families, many pioneers in the field of family therapy, many years being a clinical member of the American Association of Marriage and Family Therapy, the American Counseling Association and the American Psychological Association, attending seminars with pioneers in these fields, and reading and studying the literature from all of these fields. I have come to believe the family tries its best and that parents can influence children more than anyone. However, the family members can sabotage this influential power by letting the addictive behavior 'get to them' and allowing themselves to let this problem go until the anger builds and they reject the addict. This is the number one pitfall. I intend to show you how to avoid this. I have learned the right things to say, how and when to say them, how much to say and when to stop talking. I'll share all of this with you in this book.

Three years later, 1968 to be precise, I was teaching high school when one of my students died due to ingestion of Pam (inhalant) that froze her lungs. I'll spare you the details. At that moment, I realized that I wanted to work in the field of counseling. I found my "calling" in life. Since that day I have been studying and practicing and learning and keeping up with my field and I don't regret a moment of it. I have been blessed with being a part of many recoveries. This is my "calling" in life. I have learned to accept this challenge – working with people who are afflicted with the disease of addiction. It has its upside and its downside.

Believe me when I tell you, I know how hard it is to watch this problem in your own home with your precious child. I also know how difficult it is for an addict to stop and then change radically. This is the downside. On the other hand, there is the upside. We learn the tools of recovery as long as we are teachable. I have had to adapt to recovery. It is a lifestyle, not something to do for a year or so like a college degree. There is no graduation. This disease is there for life. But I also know the "joy of living" that is the outgrowth of the 'gift' of recovery.

Back in 1986, when I started finding out what real recovery is and how it works, I listened to a recovering alcoholic by the name of Jim W. from Texas. He started out by saying that he was sober 21 years at the time. Then he continued to say he drank martinis. He described the ingredients in a martini and went on to say that "one would taste good right now." Well, I was pretty surprised to realize that he had a temptation after all that time. This insight let me realize that this phenomenon does not go away. Since that time, I have seen this, read it and believe it.

This disease will trick you into thinking it is gone. 'It has a life of its own.' This is a vital piece of information that forms the cornerstone of the treatment process: it can be arrested but does not go away. It requires ongoing maintenance. Believe me when I tell you this! This information is tried and true and based on my experience and also throughout valid recovery literature. I seldom base a conclusion only on my solo experience. I believe in research that is rigorous and methodologically sound, not surveys or weak studies with many design errors.

Therefore, treatment (twelve-step work) must be ongoing. Learn this from me. I hope that you do not learn this the hard way. It's easier if you trust me. Look at the research for yourself. Do your own research also. Go where recovering people are. Go where the families are. You'll see the success. Some have tried to recover on their own and will tell you the pitfalls and pain that 'going it on your own' fosters. I literally hear these stories of failure every other day. The good news is that recovery, the addict/alcoholic's and the family's individual recovery is not hard or difficult. Hard and difficult are words that sabotage you. They are negative and can 'program' you into failing. Throw them out. Look at the issue as being "uncharted waters." The information and manner of handing the problem is NEW. New is easy to digest as it is not a judgmental position. It implies that we are merely learning another way of looking at the problem. This is what we have to do. We have to be 'open' to learning and not rigid and inflexible.

We have to help you, your child, and your family change thoughts, feelings and actions, actually reverse them, so as to combat the damage and turn around this dark force. This takes about three years of work to begin and a lifetime to keep. At first, this is intense. Feelings rise and the damage done by the disease has to be resolved. After a few months, treatment continues but you should be attending twelve-step meetings more and practicing new behaviors, thoughts and feelings in the mainstream of life. Therapy needs to be consistent, persistent and committed. Not everyone, in fact hardly anyone, will do this. It still needs to be done. Be the one to do it. And one word of caution - don't be a "crisis junky," only getting help when desperate. It can be a trap that is debilitating. Learn how to cope with recovery on a committed and consistent daily basis and thus avoid crises and enjoy life.

The Wrong Way

I have treated early stage alcoholics/addicts, middle stage and late stage alcoholics and poly-substance addicts since the 1960's. While working in a locked inpatient hospital in western New York I learned the wrong theory, methods and techniques for treating drug addiction and alcoholism. The theory used there was that addiction is caused by 'acting out' on buried feelings. This theory implied that if we regulate and resolve our built up aggression, fear, guilt and hurts, we could resist addiction, actually overcome it. This is preposterous as it does not account for cravings, loss of control, and the progression of the illness (to other drugs and higher doses) or tolerance. The disease is not based on psychological underpinnings. It continues because the addict cannot quit on his own.

In fact, I tried to quit for 10 years by myself and would have if I could have. So would millions of others who have incredible will power except in this area. It was very valuable to learn the wrong way because it let me know what doesn't work (the group leader was getting drunk every month and actually landed in jail) and motivated me to find what does work. I am positive that I now know what does and does not work. My prior experience was very useful, probably the most important learning I could get. Now I try to learn without making mistakes or suffering. Besides, I have made many mistakes so you can learn from me and not have to make these mistakes. I can also now learn what not to do from those who still 'fight' successful recovery methods and learn what to do from those who do it the right way.

My next job was supervising a suicide prevention and intervention component of a mental health center that also specialized in drug and alcohol treatment. Most of our staff in this and the former treatment center were using drugs and alcohol abusively if not addictively. There I learned all about untreated addiction and what damage simply not using could do. Good people do have this pre-genetic disposition for addiction and even work in the addiction field or in any other field for that matter. This is common. Addiction is an "equal opportunity disease." It equally affects doctors, lawyers, presidents, teachers, athletes and so forth. This awareness can show you that denial exists in all addicts no matter how functional or dysfunctional we are. We have more in common than not.

During my early stages of addiction when there were few serious or consistent problems, Jimi Hendrix, Janis Joplin, Jim Morrison, Elvis and countless other well known public figures overdosed and died. I even saw an addict die in my arms at the age of 20. This did not influence me to consider stopping. As is true even now, over 50 years later, there was no one who got sober and spoke out against addiction. There was and still is a stigma to addiction. People don't get clean and sober and 'speak out.' There are singers and actors today who get clean but, as always, do not speak out against it. Back in the 50's and 60's, it was worse however. No one was there to point the way. No one was there to model the path to recovery; no one. We need to educate families with accurate information about this disease.

As above, celebrities get sober but, as a rule, are quiet about it. They err on the side of caution. This disease is a silent killer. Even when celebrities get caught and hit a bottom, we hear little of it. The money covers it up. Politicians cover it up. The media downplays it. This has been and still is what this disease feeds off - SILENCE. The cruelest lies are often told in silence. This is why I developed the motto: "JUST SAY SOMETHING."

Further, some don't talk about addiction because they're afraid of the controversy. Some keep quiet because of fear, lack of confidence and the safety of silence. Others stay silent because they do not know the disease is causing the problem. We are taught to think that the person is crazy; the problem is mental; the death was accidental; the car crash was due to fatigue; the stomach ulcer was due to stress, and so on. The disease hides behind delusion. No one affected by it takes responsibility for their part in it. This fact is actually another variable that motivated me to write this book, create my model and develop my favorite motto and trademark phrase: "For God's sakes, Just Say Something!"

My responsibility for my behavior became apparent after I began to attend twelve-step meetings and listened to others claim responsibility for their problems and tell how they had make amends for them. My accountability lies in the fact that, when I was using, I did not want to know about the problem that I didn't think I had because I insisted on doing exactly as I wanted. I did not know the truth and did not want anyone to instruct me or control me. I thought that my drinking, pot use, cocaine use and whatever else I wanted to use was "my business." Addicts like me give off an air of standoffishness and intimidate others. We have a way of being that warns others not to invade or intrude on our addictive 'space.' This is the addict's side of the problem contributing to the stigma in society, personally and familiarly. People do not like this about us.

What my personal experience, training and education taught me was that an insidious disease such as addiction could exist almost unknown and, at the same time be pandemic, spreading false rumors about itself and telling millions that they didn't have the problem. Not only doesn't anyone I've ever met want to have it but no one wants this culprit in the family. No one! What's more, this problem causes problems ranging from embarrassment to death. It gets worse and worse until it takes over people and then homes, towns, cities.

Further, no one wants it to exist in their world. Schools don't want an addiction problem but it's there. As mentioned before, Hollywood addicts laugh at everyone else while they cover up their addictions and make incredible amounts of money being cute and making a joke out of others' efforts to publicize this dilemma. They think that they can smoke pot, drink and/or use other products and that, because they do not end up in jail on a daily basis, because their money and fame insulates them from exposure, it is ok to speak out about the benefits of using. They are ignorant of and seemingly uncaring about others, especially all of the children who need to get 'clean' and then out of urban America in order to become successes. Don't they care that these kids are trapped and that they have the power to help them get out? They don't have to give them any of their precious money or material things with which they have been blessed. All they have to do is speak out against the loser mentality that accompanies addiction. All of this 'bad publicity' reinforces the idea that the problem is minimal or, even worse, acceptable.

This corruption caused by the disease of addiction allows the problem to continue, to grow, to proliferate and to destroy. Until we educate the world with accurate information about this epidemic we will continue to live in denial and let it consume us, perhaps to our demise. Those who are not addicts simply don't understand addiction. The information that we need to deliver is that there is a difference between addiction, abuse, social use and experimental use. There is abuse that is serious but is not addiction. Abusers can quit; addicts cannot.

Motivation becomes the core issue here. The person in pain wants an opiate to relieve the pain; the addict wants to get 'high.' This means that the person with the pre-genetic disposition cannot quit but the abuser who may be using for relief can quit if the using creates problems and does not solve problems. Also, because there is a marijuana epidemic in this country, we need to spread the word that pot compromises the immune system, causes cancer, emphysema, a-motivation, impaired thinking and a plethora of other problems for the addict. We also need to let people know that alcohol is still the most lethal drug we have ever had and will continue to be until we spread the word that it kills just like crack, crystal meth and oxycontin.

Parents – if your child has this problem, get it treated.
You're not going to believe what happens next!!!
Doc Pete

My next experience lead me to the University of Central Florida in the early 1980's where I taught counseling courses to graduate counseling education students. I taught from 1980 until 1987, a year after I got sober. There I taught most of the courses to include the substance abuse (addictions) course in 1987. I was able to teach what I believed to be true based not only on my experience at twelve-step meetings, but also on my observation, counseling education and training. One of my startling discoveries came when students would reveal that they were in recovery but did not go to twelve-step meetings because they worked in the counseling "field" with addicts/alcoholics all day and this was their therapy. My studies led me to believe that, if you work with alcoholic/addicts, this calls for more meetings due to the stress and being exposed to active, newly recovered and struggling addicts.

This leads to my next point. The recovering person needs to be around recovering people often. If really dependent on substances and really an alcoholic and/or and addict, this is necessary. This is what works. Try not to reinvent the wheel. Dismiss your ideas about his recovery and do what has demonstrated effectiveness. Millions of people are sober and clean in thousands of twelve-step programs. Why would you try anything other than what works? This is true for you, your family and your son.

The lesson derived from this is that it takes humility to get and stay sober and clean. Our ideas about our problem are usually wrong. One can surely be motivated by fear to get "in" recovery but will go right back "out" (relapse) if he doesn't get humble, teachable and soon. That is why the thinking needs to change from "I know what to do" to "I know enough to get me to a meeting." Arrogance, "know-it-all-it is," has to vanish. The arrogant thinking has to be countered by the tragic 'bottom' that 'puts the addict in his place.' Nagging and coaxing and pleading do not get someone sober and clean. It usually takes a near-death experience to reach the 'bottom' that changes the person's mind and softens the pride so that the person can get humble. The ultimate risk is to detach when you, as the parent, know of this danger and create the awareness for your child that he is in danger. However, your unwillingness to sit back and watch him 'fall' can make him aware enough to take recovery action.

Think of the persistence that addicts have when fighting this 'bottom' as similar to Paul Newman's stubbornness in the movie Cool Hand Luke. George Kennedy beat the living daylights out of him and he still wouldn't surrender. He was still throwing punches after he was almost unconscious. George Kennedy carried him to his bed and quit beating on him, luckily for Paul Newman. Unfortunately or should I say fortunately, the disease of addiction does not let up or stop until the addict stops fighting, stops trying to beat it. We cannot control this problem. We have to surrender, become students, and learn from successful recovering people how to do this. We cannot "beat the game." Many addicts have died trying to do this. We cannot control cravings with our obsessed mind or power of our will, just as we can't control seizures or the flu symptoms. When we try to control a physiological phenomenon, we lose. We simply have to use the treatment that works – Surrender To Win. Use the tact that Japan did in World War ll. By surrendering, they survived near annihilation and went on to regroup and undergo a positive transformation.

Unfortunately, I have found that, across the board, there are many, many excuses to avoid what works. This is especially true of those who are in the helping profession. Many addicted therapists do not frequent twelve-step meetings. However, this is also true of lawyers, doctors, homeless people, and anyone else who thinks he can do this alone. It may have more to do with one's pride and misguided thinking than anything else. It is very, very difficult for many addicts to admit that they cannot manage by self alone. This autonomy is important when playing any solo sport, test-taking, driving and performing any other activity that calls for independence. On the other hand, when it comes to the disease of addiction, autonomy does not work. Even doctors are warned against treating themselves. The sick mindset is that they are helpers and not helpees. I learned that one cannot treat a sick mind with a sick mind. Because of this, it is very difficult, if not impossible, for the alcoholic/addict to help oneself.

It is equally difficult to ask for help. I find this to be true of myself. My pride has and still can get in the way. I do it anyways - ask for and use help - because I no longer entertain the thought of going it alone. I tried this in my thirties for ten years and I hope I learned my lesson. In recovery,

I have been given a new life and the awareness to know it. As a result, I am consistently relieved to be functioning and inspired to live the best life I can. I have to be thinking of ways to repay for my reprieve each day. Otherwise, there are recovery traps everywhere.

Creating the 'Bottom'

This disease has so many deceptive corridors that it's a wonder anyone gets sober. I think that we've even had alcoholic Presidents and no one really knew or bothered to intervene. However, there is a way to success. Gratitude and giving back to others who suffer from this illness are tools that neutralize and help us to rise above the self-centeredness and self-pity of the disease. This change from defiance to surrender is difficult to do if one still has health, wealth, brains and good looks. These can serve as the basis for rationalizing why the addict is not affected by the use. These material qualities can be the measures of success in spite of spiritual, moral, psychological and/or emotional bankruptcy.

If one values the 'material world' over the spiritual, it is almost impossible to get sober. Power, fame, money – all of these can lead to pride and a sense of self creation that makes it very, very difficult to swallow one's pride and admit to so-called, albeit necessary admission of failure. This is why the creation of the 'bottom' is so vital. It leads to the needed humility and the newfound ability and willingness to 'break denial' - admit the loss of control and problems associated with using. It is the perception of the problem (bottom) that matters. I have seen many people get sober because their child cried and many die of addiction after being told by their doctor that they would die if they 'went back out.' However, parents can be the answer. Parents can help the child feel the pain by letting them know of the pain they, the parents, are in as a result of the addiction. This can touch the heart of a child if you do it before it's too late.

Accurate Diagnosis

While teaching at UCF, I knew I was giving accurate information about addiction because I had done the research, lived it and learned the truth at my meetings. I also read the brochures and fact sheets of drug and alcohol treatment centers that boasted a high success rate and wondered about the efficacy of their reports. I became curious about treatment outcomes and wondered how they obtained their numbers. My later studies at the University of Florida helped me to be able to understand research design and validity and reliability standards. This helped me to further back up my reports and statistics gleaned from studies with valid, reliable and rigorous research. I had just finished my research for my dissertation on addiction relapse prevention and could also apply this to my teaching. My work regarding research and design error was especially valuable as it helped me to measure treatment effectiveness. Later I used this knowledge to start my first treatment center. I now believe that treatment does not cure your child. God dose and we must lead him to Him.

My education and experience in mental health also lead me to develop expertise in this area. Having a strong background in mental health, I could tell when the problem was addiction and when it was mental health, organic, social, family or a combination. This has been a great advantage in my work as I could see that addiction, true addiction, mimics many other problems. Addiction causes many problems to include depression, mania, anxiety, family dysfunction, social anxiety and so forth. All addicts suffer from psychological damage or else they wouldn't be addicts. This is true by definition. It is my belief that many of these problems are transient and usually dissipate or disappear with time away from the intoxicants. It is a mistake to treat these problems with medication early in recovery unless the person is highly suicidal, i.e., serious intent and prior history with plans and a method, availability of method, is obviously mentally ill, has physical problems or has relapsed because of these problems. This of course begs the question of how would one know if these concerns cause relapse or treatment failure. One mistake to avoid is to insulate the addict from the problems by taking care of them for him, medicating them, putting him in treatment and preventing the aforementioned 'bottom' from occurring and thus aid in keeping the addict from the pain and loss needed to recover.

It is the obligation of the "Helping field" to give you the best service available, treatment that is based on valid and reliable information, delivered by professionals who have the skills, knowledge and abilities required to provide you and your family with the best service available.

Accurate diagnosis must involve a team or someone well versed in disciplines such as mental health, psychiatry, psychology and addiction. My studies of these have helped me to diagnose accurately. At times, I have deferred a second diagnosis or a dual or co-occurring disorder because of conflicting symptoms, a need for detoxification or symptom confusion. I have been able to see beyond the tunnel vision that occurs when training is limited to one area. If you study only addiction, it is difficult to see a co-occurring disorder. If your training is medical then drugs may be the only answer. If you are a carpenter, everything looks like a board… Training needs to be multidisciplinary. This attitude and caution has been invaluable and I believe has made the difference between recovery and death on many occasions.

Summary

To summarize, this book is my attempt to share what I believe, have seen work and give you ways to approach the problem successfully. In this book, for the first time, I have combined my experiences in the workplace, on the 'front lines' as a counselor, my personal experience of 25 years of using, my personal recovery since 1986 (7-11-86) without a drink or a drug and my education to include a Ph.D. and a dissertation on relapse prevention with alcoholics and addicts. For the past 45 years I have been learning about addiction 'as a student' and have seen it from the recovering user's eyes also. I have seen much success, much relapse, many overdoses and much death due to this evil phenomenon. I have seen it takes lives without killing and ruin marriages, souls, families, destroy egos and take away jobs. It wants the addict/alcoholic dead but will be satisfied with us getting high or drunk because then it knows that it will destroy others and eventually consume us, have its way with us. I know this problem backwards and forwards and know that an intense study of accurate information about it followed by appropriate actions can lead to success. However, you must do this according to directions. No other way works as well. I know these directions and can teach them. Join me on the journey. As above, I have seen people try to recover by using their thinking. Many didn't make it but some did. Some died and some suffered because they did not grow and the untreated mind, feelings and actions did not change. They continued to harm others, lie, cheat and steal and were miserable. I have seen others hide behind religion and be ok on Sundays but be the same old person Monday to Saturday. Some did well but I have not seen this often. God bless you if you can get sober another way. I have an easier and more successful way than I could have ever imagined.

CHAPTER FIVE

FAMILY RECOVERY MODEL

A functional addictive family is an oxymoron.
Doc Pete

The journey continues. Read and learn how the family can heal. Read closely and see how we can do this together.

Actually, addiction has two components that are relevant to family treatment. First and foremost is the realization that the addict's problem is characterized by defiance stemming from the fear of not getting high. This can keep a person from learning, doing what is necessary to recover. It keeps an addict from being honest. In order to recover one must have the courage to see reality honestly. He may find out that the problem is worse than he thought. He will learn that he has a part in the problem. This also has relevance for family members. When the family knows the defiance isn't personal, they don't have to personalize the harm done. Second is the fact that this is a family problem and that all members have been affected. With family treatment healing can occur.

The Family's Path

The alcoholic/addict uses the drug. The family members (parents) react at first to protect the addict and later by trying to control the problem, the addict, as they feel shamed and fearful, protective as well as frustrated and guilty. The user justifies the using behavior or blames someone or something and the parents become more astonished by the audacity of the user. The addict may try to quit and even explain that he has stopped many times and that he can quit whenever he wants. This thinking is typical of the addict and attempts must immediately be made to stop and correct this rationalization. Your response could suggest that quitting, by definition, only happens once. Questioning or advising him will not help.

The problem is that your child will not listen until he feels the pain and loss associated with his using. This is a reversal of the thought process that he has as he is minimizing the problems that occur from his using. Our goal is the reversal of thought process that the drug and/or alcohol use is creating problems. You can help him see this. This has to and does occur frequently in treatment. However, we can create this 'bottom' in the home by adhering to our agreement that there are consequences for breaking the rules. Give him boundaries and not lectures.

The Family's Path

At this point, we cannot allow his thinking to sabotage treatment entry efforts. Eventually, when the family goes to treatment, the family members get better and detach with love from the rescuing behavior. Otherwise, they risk becoming as sick if not sicker than the alcoholic/addict. The grief, frustration, hurt, guilt and/or fear multiply and infect the entire household if no treatment occurs. Family therapists speak of the family unit as being a 'system' that is affected by the actions of all of its members. Conversely so and on a positive note, when a family member goes to treatment and begins to heal, other members are affected, usually in a positive way. There is a correlation between parents who attend Al-Anon and children who adopt this way of life, go to meetings and recover. Children have a tendency to do what their parents do. Remember when he was five and repeated what you said, sang the same songs, used the same words, walked the same ways, told the same jokes later on and used the same expressions as you? Well, he still will.

Stages and rationalizations

I want to caution you regarding a subtle fact about addiction that can be very confusing to the average person and can deceive the family into thinking that the problem is minimal. The fact is that there are different stages of addiction. These are determined by frequency and duration of use. There are also genetic factors, genetic loadings, that I believe affect different addicts in different ways. These manifest in confusing ways and appear in some addicts in a comparative sense. In other words, it may seem as though some addicts have a 'milder dose' of addiction whereas they actually have progressed at a slower rate than an addict who may have larger genetic loadings for addiction. The fact is that the disease progresses differently for different addicts. The typical addict, looking for any reason to continue using, can use this phenomenon to explain why he has his disease under control. Many addicts will compare their use to a peer's use, especially if the peer has progressed further. As a parent, it is important to be aware of this dynamic and not be swayed into thinking that your child is 'better off' than a peer and, therefore, capable of delaying or dismissing treatment because he is not that bad off. Early intervention is important. The following explains the stages.

The following table lists and explains the seven stages and how to use these to motivate.

TABLE 3 - STAGES OF ADDICTION

At times, addicts and/or alcoholics do not progress uniformly in their disease. There are stages. By knowing the stages, you will have a better idea of how and when to intervene and what strategies to implement in order to get him to treatment.

Stages overlap and may not occur at all. For example, some addicts/alcoholics transition from Active Addiction to Decision without going through Pre-treatment or Defiance. Some transition from Active Addiction to Active (recovery) after they have almost died and are aware of the problem (bottom) and still care. These get motivated to take the strong actions needed for continued recovery. Whatever the case, present the problems that you see and feel consistently. Do not allow the disease to live in your house unnoticed. The following are a list and description of these stages:

---

1. Active addiction – denial with no thoughts of stopping; can't see problems. Forced help may be harmful. Self-disclose. Call him on consequences (See Intervention model). Your Al-Anon participation helps him to see the problems.

2. Pre-treatment – denial stage yet he may have glimpses of problem areas but minimizes them. Pressured help may be harmful. Self-disclose and hold him accountable. Al-Anon helps you to be consistent, i.e., hold him accountable.

3. Defiance – awareness of problems with argument and/or ambivalence. He still has a need to control his use and will "go on the wagon" for a while but cannot feel the impact of the consequences yet. Self-disclose about your fears and frustrations. He may stop temporarily "for others" and then eventually for himself.

4. Decision – Decision to change is made but commitment may not be strong. Support and point out problems to him as your consequences. Get help!

5. Action – Steps are made to begin stopping the problem. Continued support is needed with positive reinforcement of his recovery. Do whatever it takes to help him connect with recovering peers and treatment.

6. Vigilance – Initial changes are made. Relapse prevention is the goal. Encourage.

7. Relapse – Return to Program or suffer. Self-disclose and Intervene.

Butkins © 2012

Family Resistance

To restate, all of the family members need to heal. All members need to be involved in treatment. However, there is usually resistance to family treatment also, either initially or during the process. Many people who are affected by addiction and who do not use drugs or alcohol but have lived with an addict cope in maladaptive ways. They have to somehow cope with the pain of family addiction. Some play sports and hurt others to sublimate their rage and fears. Others become workaholics to avoid feelings and get a sense of achievement. Others develop 'soft' addictions such as gambling, overeating or spending. In all cases, the feelings are left buried and the co-addict 'acts out' in these ways. When the co-addicts heal the pain softens and resistance is minimal. When untreated, families hold onto the familiar. Depression usually occurs.

As above, this discouragement can result in treatment resistance and come in the form of stopping or avoiding treatment, canceling therapy sessions or not cooperating in other ways. In addition, many times when things become more stable, the family quits treatment. This can be resistance to deal with the pain of recovery even though it seems that healing is completed. This is a mistake. Although this is normal as the tendency is to control the situation, it is dangerous and leads to treatment failure. Resistance is usually fear or old feelings of rebellion and distorted thinking. The disease breeds fear and anger that leads to defiance. These feelings must be 'countered' with courage and strength from a higher source and others who know this problem and have recovered. The right action is to keep doing what is works. If your child is abstinent, treatment is working. Now we have to work on the areas that have been harmed by the disease. Much work needs to be done. The 'difficult' or new part may be changing the negative behaviors and feelings and thoughts. The transformation that is needed takes time, about three years and then needs to be maintained over a lifetime. However, you should see some change very soon if they attend twelve-step meetings often. Also, trust the treatment staff which has been so helpful. They know the traps such as leaving treatment early and can guide you as you walk through the healing process.

Self-reliance and Treatment Failure

Has it seemed as though you've lost your child? You're among many if you have. What do you do? Can you imagine your home being back to normal when you were close as a family? Follow my lead and we'll get you back there. Now, I'm going to explain what I have learned to be the NUMBER ONE PITFALL THAT LEADS TO FAILURE: Again, this involves attempting my model YOUR way and not MY way. This results in relapse, the return to crisis state, and the return of hopelessness and all of the other negatives this problem brings. You and your family can become 'crisis junkies' and get caught up in this circular process until it takes you, all of you, out of the picture or you decide to do this my way. This is but one of the problems that can keep you from following directions. I have the solution but you have to follow the path I outline.

Men are notorious for sabotaging their success by a need to do it 'my way' when it should be done the way that is "Tried and TRUE". This is because of the 'reptile brain' that says we must be the hunter, the provider, the manager, the one in control. Women have a maternal instinct that is biological. This instinct is characterized by a strong desire to nurture and care for another. Both of these male/female traits can lead to undermining of the plan. When addiction affects these parents' children there is a tremendous desire to control long after it has ceased to be effective. As above, this can evolve into a desperate attempt to fix the problem in spite of evidence of the futility of this direction. There is another way that works. Follow this way! When we learn to follow another who knows this way, we can reach our goal. Remember, you are taking a journey comparable to a walk through the Amazon. Without a guide the results are dangerous and at times disastrous, even fatal. You know the dangers of this journey. Believe me when I tell you that the journey of recovery has the same traps, the same vipers, crocodiles and quicksand as the jungle. View this journey as a life-saving venture in which you must cooperate or lose your family, self-respect and maybe a life.

Follow my model (see Table 2 below) as prescribed and I'll show you the way out. The following is my outline of this model:

TABLE 4 - FAMILY RECOVERY MODEL – RELAXED

1. Recognition of the problem.

2. Embrace the Relationship with your child.

3. Look, identify, observe the problem.

4. Alternatives - strategize, plan the direction.

5. X factor – Intervention plan.

6. Entry to treatment.

7. Defense and maintenance of recovery.

Butkins © 2012

The above model is based on what I have learned over my lifespan in order to help you succeed like so many that I have helped. Keep in mind that your child needs us to direct him as he is not capable of doing this himself. It is my sincerest desire that you allow me to assist you in doing so. If you could have got him sober you would have. I know you have tried everything you can think of to help him. I have studied and practiced for many years to develop systems that work. I can teach these to you.

The following seven chapters explain each step of the model in order. Pay close attention to the order of these steps as well as to the content. Use these chapters as study guides. Take your time and we'll use this as a way to get out of the problem.

CHAPTER SIX

RECOGNITION - STEP 1

Don't be afraid to see what you see.
Ronald Reagan

Pay close attention to your child's attitude, feelings and his behavior! Now that you have seen drug or alcohol use by your child, ask yourself the question, "What am I really looking at?" Take another look at the concern and study what you have seen. Unless you have 'been there' this problem can be difficult to see. Has the problem progressed or is it beginning? Have you been through this before? Is this a relapse – a period after a lapse from recovery - or was your child never in recovery? Analyze the situation. Study Table 5 and check off or circle the behaviors you have seen or that you suspect or have been told.

TABLE 5 - HOW CAN YOU TELL IF YOUR TEEN IS USING DRUGS?

Warning Signs

Suddenly avoids contact with the family.

Experiences rapid mood swings.

Steals money from family, friends or others.

Becomes defiant.

New friends are older or less suitable to the family.

New friends are known to use drugs.

School conduct becomes a problem.

Drop in grades is unexplained.

Develops an apathetic attitude toward being successful.

Tends to isolate.

Withdrawal from former hobbies or sports.

Some of the things you will see:

More illness, running nose, cough, dilated pupils, red eyes, slurred speech, lethargy, apathy (little interest in success in appearance, school or activities which were formerly of interest to your child), smell of marijuana in room or on the child, trance-like state, disorientation, hyperactivity followed by drowsiness, nausea, loss of coordination, loss of appetite, headaches/hangover, red nostrils, slowed speech, absentmindedness, weight gain, fatigue, staggering walk.

Some of the things you will find:

Paraphernalia such as pipes, rolling papers, roach clips, empty cigars, cans with a hole in the side, needles, cellophane bags with foreign powder or brown/green stems, seeds, smelly, sticky grass or fine granular smelly substance, glues bottles or aerosol cans, razor blades, ashes on the floor, pills or capsules, pill bottles, long fingernails (especially only the pinky), any foreign papers or objects, powder on nose, and any unusual clothing patterns which display drugs or known drug users. Lastly, look for friendships with new persons whom you suspect for any reason.

Butkins © 2012

These are the symptoms which are the most prevalent, observable and frequent. These, especially when observed in groups of three or four, can be strong signs of drug abuse. Do not let these signs go unattended. Get help as soon as you can in order to begin the process of reconstruction. There is hope. Ask questions of knowledgeable persons at the police station or treatment centers if you are unfamiliar with any of the above.

Do not panic! Seek help.

Partnership and Recognition

Next, talk to your spouse or 'significant other.' If you are not in a committed relationship or your current relationship is not friendly, perhaps there is another child, relative or good friend who is mature enough to partner with and to talk with and process the situation. Again, this could also be a good time to see a therapist. Remember, this could be life or death! Drug and alcohol deaths are reported in the media every day. Do not delay. You must strike while the 'iron is hot.' Plan to meet with your 'partner' for the sole purpose of discussing your child's abuse of drugs and/or alcohol. Relate just what it is you both have seen. Discuss the issues and compare notes on the above list. Give each other time to talk. Do not interrupt and be patient. Compare notes once more. What are the behaviors? Is your child coming home late, sleeping in, and becoming apathetic about work or school? Is your child staggering when they come home? Are his pupils dilated? Is he lying, cheating or stealing? Are his friends not suitable? Use the table below, Table 6, to again review behaviors. What are you seeing? Review your position by using the checklist below as a guide. Check off the behaviors you have seen.

TABLE 6 – TYPICAL DRUG/ALCOHOL BEHAVIORS:

Substance Abuse Signs and Symptoms: Parents Don't Have To Be The Last To Know!

Family/Social Behavior

- Change in Attitude toward rules, parents, brothers, and sisters
- Isolating (staying in room...)
- Breaking curfew, sneaking out, becoming more secretive, making excuses for late hours
- Lying (blaming others for irresponsible actions)
- Violence (physical and/or verbal)
- Erratic Sleeping/eating habits (too much or too little)
- Evasiveness about company kept and where time was spent
- Unusual telephone calls (parties hang up or refuse to be identified)
- DUI's, unusual car accidents, extreme wear and tear on car, dents, tickets
- Unreasonable resentments, attitudes
- Suspicion of money or alcohol missing from parents or family members
- Stealing and/or selling possessions to be pawned for money (clothing, records, gifts, etc.)
- Manipulating parents: playing one against the other
- Has money but no job
- Has job, but always needs more money
- Values conflict, i.e. lying, stealing, etc., stops going to church/temple, family functions, meals, etc.

Friends and Peer Group

- Change in peer group with little interest in old friends
- New friends have drug user reputation
- Parents don't know friends and can't get names or addresses
- Begins to associate with an older crowd

School/Social Behavior

- Sudden or gradual drop in grades and achievement (reasons unclear)
- Skipping classes or entire days, tardiness
- Disrespect or defiance toward teachers, rules, and regulations
- Present in classroom, but inattentive
- Frequent suspensions/expulsions/fights
- Shoplifting
- Delinquent behavior
- Difficulty studying or working at job or 'on the job' absenteeism
- Denies knowledge of or ownership of paraphernalia
- Possession of alcohol or drugs at school
- Suspicion or reports of being 'under the influence' at school

Change in Physical/Psychological Condition

- Emotional state changes rapidly
- Weight changes (drastic loss or gain)
- Changes in speech pattern (slurred speech)
- Burns on hands or clothing
- Withdrawal from healthy peers
- Very defensive
- Stumbling, confusion, disorientation
- Mood and/or personality changes
- Obsession and preoccupation with chemicals
- Denial, minimizing, blaming, rationalizing, intellectualizing
- Attention span shorter
- Blackouts (amnesia about recent past)
- Wearing clothes with drug symbols

General

- Lack of response or concern expresses regarding any of the above

Is your partner seeing the same things? If so, you're probably "reading" the situation accurately. If you're both objective, this is probably accurate information. Assess the severity. Is he using without seeming consequences, typifying initial stages? Is he having problems and continuing use, thus typifying middle stage? Are there physical problems, suggesting late, chronic stages? The more advanced, the worse he is. Use these indicators to get an accurate 'read' of the problem. Try not to minimize.

Is this a Medical Concern?

Is your child using or does he or she have the flu, sinus problems, an infection or another medical condition? Rule this in or out. If a medical condition, find a medical solution. See a Doctor of medicine. Keep a close eye to make sure that the problem is just medical. Those who use drugs and/or alcohol tend to hide the symptoms of using behind many things. It's not unusual for someone to use and have a medical problem. Look for both. Always err on the side of caution. Err on the side of mistrust because the disease infects the user so that he can't be trusted to tell the truth. Further, as above, the disease mimics many other problems. Do not be naive. This disease feeds on this. If medical, treat the medical problem. Could the problem be a grief reaction to a loss that seems to be a depression? Could it be an abusive trend due to a loss or a phase that many teens go through as a part of their development? These are factors you have to rule in or out.

Is it a Mental Health Concern?

Again, see an expert in this field. Get advice and counsel from a trained professional. By this I mean someone who had been there and is in recovery and has been trained to evaluate and treat addiction as well as differentiate addiction from another issue. In addition, make sure you have your child take a psychological inventory after he is sober and clean for a few weeks, especially if you think or are told that there may be another problem. This instrument plus a clinical inventory and other testing can tell you if there is another problem. Don't take the word of someone who diagnoses another problem while your child is detoxifying, however. How can anyone diagnose another problem while your child is still 'toxified' unless it is extreme or was there before he started using? I don't think this makes much sense at all. After he is sober and clean, the testing can be a strong indicator of whether there is a co-occurring disorder such as a major depression, a bi-polar problem, an anxiety disorder or any other type of disorder. If severe depression, anxiety or any other psychological problem is getting in the way of your recovery, address this.

I have seen many people with moderate to severe mental 'health problems' get sober and clean without medication. However, I have seen dozens of addicts get on or stay on or increase their medications in order to get high. Of course, they could not admit that they were getting a euphoric effect (high) because they were high. There is something suspect about an addict not considering other methods of coping before ingesting a drug that has been his downfall or that could lead to a drug that kills him. Many of these people I have seen do this died due to the intoxicants. One was an ex-girlfriend; one was a good friend; others were acquaintances that I knew in or out of the recovery rooms.

Recovery must come first. It must be number one. Addiction is a PRIMARY PROBLEM and must be treated first. Other problems must be carefully investigated before medication is used. Alternate strategies for healing physical pain, loss and grief… must be investigated. Remember, addicts need to be in strong recovery or closely monitored if given mood-altering chemicals. Further, the addict can easily go back to getting high on prescription medications and rationalize it. The family can easily go along with this because they 'don't want the problem' anyway and can also fall into denial again. Ask me how I know.

Next you will need to gather more information by talking with your child. The purpose is to find out what his thoughts are. Is he in denial or not? This involves talking to him or her in a way that is effective. This is an "art" and absolutely necessary. Before you do this, study the defenses that may get in the way of an accurate assessment.

Defense Mechanisms

Minimizing is one of the defense mechanisms used to avoid recognizing the extent of this awful disease, primarily because we do not want it in the family. Who would? It comes under the umbrella of justification and is a form of denial. All are affected by this disease, either directly (user) or indirectly (family) to include the parents, siblings, other relatives and the addict/alcoholic. The tendency to rationalize, intellectualize, blame others and/or use other avoidance techniques interferes with the ability to see the truth for both the addict and the family. The purpose these defenses serve is to 'assist the disease' in not being discovered. If you can think of addiction as having a life of its own, you can begin to realize that it wants everyone around it dead and especially the addict/alcoholic but usually settles for getting them drunk and high again. See the addiction for what it is. Note the signs and symptoms that you see and compare with your partner. You can keep each other out of denial. Remember, the disease wants all to remain in denial and that includes you. In this first stage of discovery, it is of utmost importance not to be distracted from what you really see by the child's defenses. Don't be deceived. Remember, this disease can be fatal!

Accurate Information

So, hopefully by now, you can see that it is easy to be fooled by this concern. Make sure you are evaluating this by reasonable and normal standards. For example, any drug use is serious. Drinking or 'drug use' in spite of a problem is very serious. Problems include you being afraid or angry at his behaviors, his truancy, lying, erratic thinking, emotional outbursts, his depression, and so forth. If the behavior is repeated after there is a problem; this is a problem. This is usually addiction. As before, children who are using alcohol and going through a "phase" usually will stop when there is a problem. This is not addiction. When the family is disrupted by the using and it continues, this is a problem. When the girlfriend objects or is irritated with the behavior and it continues, it's a problem. A DUI along with continued drinking and driving is a problem; it's a crime. Try to see that, unless the person using is really attached to the drug or the alcohol, he will not desire to do it again. He may even be repulsed by the behavior and the consequence. The addict will continue to repeat using because there is a physical craving and a mental obsession that is governed by the brain. This is the "key" to understanding addiction.*

It is at this point that you and your partner will be gathering information that will help determine your course of action, how to talk to your child. One of your chief indicators of addiction is what your child says. If he admits to the problem, this is strong validation. Few people have a motive for thinking they are an addict/alcoholic unless they are. You want to find out his opinion and attitude. What is his position on this subject? Further, if you talk to him when he is hung over, he may be more motivated to be motivated because there is relevant pain. If he resists, you must have a plan (More on this in a later section). Be aware not to try to help him by talking to him when he is intoxicated. *

The most important action to take now is to detach from your desire or even obsession to fix and analyze/study him. I'm not going to ask you to stop trying. However, pay attention to your frustration, fears and hurt as well as guilt. You have to be talking about these feelings, especially the anger, before it lingers and builds up. As above, you can become obsessed with this desire to help. Get help before this "other-focused" position turns into an obsession. This involves recognizing this preoccupation as being counter-productive. Work to change self. Resist the temptation to 'fix' him or try to get him to change at this point. You have to avoid denying or minimizing this as this occurs in every chemical dependent family. Many co-addicts progress to the level where they cannot stop trying to analyze or fix the addict even when asked not to do this. This can lead to mental and emotional deterioration and hospitalization.

The Co-addict's Obsession

I want to expand on this potential pitfall so you can avoid it when trying to help your child. This is an important issue all throughout the model. I mention it often as a reminder because it is so prevalent among families with this concern and is a major pitfall that can sabotage all of our work. Becoming obsessed with helping someone who is not accepting help can be maddening as well as futile. Because of this, the direction that you must follow includes processing your feelings of frustration and hurt (that lead to hopelessness and depression) and getting emotionally healthy. Otherwise, your feelings will generate thoughts based on the latter emotions and you will become "flooded" with 'out of control' feelings (fear and anger) that prevent you from being logical and lead to emotional outbursts. This is where you can do harm. Your words need to be based on caring and commitment to self and family. You must be logical.

Table 7 explains the results when there are combinations of parents and child either wanting to control the situation on their own or seeking help sincerely. The results are depicted in the middle rectangles. The outer labels represent the child's position (left column) and the parents' position (top two). The inner rectangle where the child's parents' positions intersect explains the results. The ideal position is when we have a help-seeking child and a help-seeking parent. We then can have recovery.

TABLE 7 – PARENT/CHILD ATTITUDES LEADING TO RECOVERY OR OTHER ALTERNATIVES

	AUTONOMOUS PARENT	**HELP-SEEKING** PARENT
AUTONOMOUS Child	**Probable Relapse**	Intervention
HELP-SEEKING Child	Strengthen Extended Family & Support System = Recovery	Definite Recovery Potential

Autonomous = raised to be independent and abide only by the methods that have made them successful, e.g., career, work ethic, exercise and being helpful with others.

Help-seeking = teachable; open to directions and willing to change. Aware that recovery is a new language and a new set of guidelines and is willing to learn and use them; knows that recovery is new to them.

The addict/alcohol needs to feel cared about and also know that he cannot manipulate you. This is a difficult line to walk. If you can be logical by resolving unpleasant feelings, you can be influential. If you react with fear, anger, guilt and hurt, you will send a message of blame, desperateness and guilt. The feelings must be expelled by talking and finishing your "unfinished business" with professional help. Otherwise, excuse yourself and have someone else to talk to him. I told you this was going to take humility. Remember, we are trying to influence and not control. Anger and frustration lead to a tendency to control. We need to influence your child to help him see that he needs help and may die without it. He needs to take action, the same as we. This is the final goal: to help your child get help for self because he wants it.* We must lead him to this mindset without force and with his cooperation. If we want it more than he does, we are in danger of being co-dependent. We may try to get him sober and clean while we get sicker and sicker. Then we become addicted to this process just as he became addicted to his drug. Hopefully, you can now see how the addiction can affect the entire family. This is the merry-go-round that we are on. Let's get off of it.

Review

Summarize exactly what you have seen and been told with each other. Write down the commonalities, differences and new findings. At this point, if you haven't already done so, it may be important to speak with a trained therapist. Make sure to choose someone who has expertise in recognizing adolescent addiction signs and symptoms. My website www.myfreedomquest.com has a section on signs and symptoms that will help you even more to complete this phase comprehensively. The conclusion of part one, Recognition of the Problem, leads to the next step in the procedure – Embracing The Relationship.

There has never been a child who could
override a strong set of parents.
Doc Pete

CHAPTER SEVEN

EMBRACE THE RELATIONSHIP - STEP 2

Be careful that you don't "love him to death."
Anonymous.

Part two of the model - The Relationship - is, like the other parts, vital to our success. This step addresses how to salvage, rekindle or maintain the connection that you currently have with your child. Here we work on the relationship. I think that one of the most important considerations for success is the condition of your relationship with your child at this time. In counseling, the therapeutic relationship accounts for 35% of the success. When parenting an addicted child, the relationship is even more important because you are the target of all of your teen's adolescent struggles.

Base your approach to repairing or enhancing the relationship on your knowledge of your child. You know him best. In addition, later on in the RELAXED Model, you will see how treatment will be based on his individual needs. We will determine what approach is best? We will also find out what approach to which he will respond and with whom he will respond best. Will he respond to 'tough love' or 'spoon-fed' treatment? Is he passive, compliant or defiant? Be confident and decide these variables based on your experience with him. Just make sure he knows that you love him. More on this in later chapters.

Now take another look at what you have seen and heard based on the information gathered in step one. Step back and get a good read on the relationship. Has he distanced you? Have you lost your child? If so, it takes a certain mindset to cope with this. This is not your fault. I will show you how to be logical and business-like yet also have a caring attitude in order to get him back. Firm attitude and tone with a confident voice tone and neutral facial expression is needed. This approach has worked for countless families and I want to share it with you. I even have a CD that gives you power statements you can use. Go to my website at: www.docpetetheimperfecttherapist.com for more information.

Due to the importance of this concept - embracing the relationship, I gave this part much serious thought before writing this chapter. I included this stage because it is often imperative that communication flows in a positive direction and because it usually does not. Therefore, you can see how important this step is.

Unfortunately, communication oftentimes becomes either lacking or heated. As stated earlier, this problem makes a parent feel powerless, the opposite of what we believe we should be, the opposite of what we want to feel. Sometimes we think that we're supposed to be in control and always in charge of our children. This doesn't work with an addicted child. Remember, addiction can be maddening. It's necessary to look at this differently. I would like for you to change this view right now. Again, I challenge you to begin to consider influencing your child instead of controlling him or her. Substitute the word influence for control. This is the first goal of this step and the most important. Control is insisting that another change; influence is helping another do something differently because it is in his best interests. Control breeds contempt; influence creates trust. Take time to learn this skill. It takes time, feedback and humility. You have to be logical, tolerant and patient. This way you can get your child back.

Guilt

In addition, keep in mind that you may be susceptible to guilt. Addicts dole out guilt trips haphazardly when they want to use. At times, it can be difficult to dodge these 'guilt trips' as they can be subtle and catch you by surprise. When these occur as they do, often and strongly at times, you may become angry or discouraged and tend to see things at their worst. Do not presume that the relationship is ruined when it is not. Again, take time to determine whether the relationship is distanced, still close or somewhere in between. Make sure that you don't overreact. Many times you can practice patience and tolerance and simply not respond to some of the guilt trips. Be aware that, although you cannot ignore every issue, you can postpone your feedback until the intervention. In addition, you can talk it out with your partner so that frustrations do not build. Emotional balance is important for this task. It is important that he sees you as a good source of information and not as someone who is overly emotional or dramatic.

Your mood and attitude affects the relationship. Sometimes it's effective to take a deep breath and slow down so that you can pause before saying something harmful. This tool can prevent you from doing great harm to the relationship. Take a rational look at the situation. What has affected your attitude? What has the addiction done to family relationships? Has it influenced other members? Are others using? The more chaotic the family, the more evidence you have that help is necessary.

Collect these experiences and observations for the intervention

There's one reason I know this part of the model so well. You can probably guess. I've been down this road so many times that I can see it in my sleep. In fact, I sometimes do. In my practice, I have worked with hundreds of addicts and alcoholics and their families. When appointments are canceled, kids offered alcohol after helping to get them sober for six months, the child reverting back to attempts to their old peer group, quitting twelve-step meetings and reverting back to control their treatment, I have become aware that the disease is controlling the actions. I have been fed up, angry, irritated, have displaced my frustration on others, been mistrustful, felt duped, conned and ready to explode or give up. I know how it feels to be on the receiving end of addictive behaviors. Therefore, I have to use the same tools that I teach. That is how I've come to know them so well. Pray for wisdom: the ability to pause before 'powering up.'

I also know what it's like to work with an addict who's just waiting for you to say something wrong so that he can then blame you. So now you can see that, once more, I have had to do what I am going to ask you to do in this situation also. I'm sure that you have 'walked on eggshells' at times, afraid to say the wrong thing for fear that he'll explode. I know that it's not easy to be in this situation but it is necessary to practice being assertive and not aggressive. We can't let our fears control our thoughts. Al-Anon helps us to learn to respond and not react. We save the negative behaviors of his using for the Intervention.

Success

On a positive note, I am happy to report that, more often than not, I have been encouraged by successful families who have taken my advice, have gone to their twelve-step meetings, kept the plan that we developed and thus were successful. Successful families learn how to treat this problem and succeed. They keep the relationship with family members and treatment staff and Al-Anon members and do not have a relationship with the disease. They 'divorce' the disease! This is necessary for success. Do not be too busy for success! Go to your meetings.

It is important to see that, even though you and your family have been compromised, harmed by the problem of addiction, in spite of this, you can still be caring. However, it has taken over your child. He has been harmed by the disease and has also been the vehicle that has done harm to you, your family and many others. Try to see that he did not choose this problem. He 'caught" it. To understand this is to cope with it. I contend that we cannot fully understand the disease unless we have had it or lived with it and have obtained accurate information. Let me attempt to explain the course of the illness.

A More In-depth Study of The Progression of the Illness – He was born this way

Some of the following has been mentioned before. However, it is important to continue to repeat the information about this otherwise confusing and treacherous problem.

The person who is using starts out using just a little as a rule, usually with peers. He does not intend to become addicted. When he drinks, for example, his body craves the substance. These cravings are about twenty times the cravings of morphine cravings (Ohlms, 1986). He does not choose these cravings. This is not his fault. He is responsible for the behaviors that ensue but, while he is unaware of his demise, he is in denial. Genetics dictate what happens for the most part. Genetic research has determined that people are predisposed to addiction (Ed. Harvard Health Publications and Shaffer, Ph.D., 2008). This means that people react differently to substances, some being unable to stop once they start.

Some normal people get drunk for the first time in high school and learn their lesson. The vomiting and hangover along with disapproval from family and friends are negative, important and therefore motivating to him. He learns from the negative consequences. He does not crave another episode because he is not compelled to use again. He does not get cravings! He does not want to use. Another child who has the genetic pre-disposition for addiction, will use in spite of much worse consequences. Even in the eye of ruination, he will keep using when it's obvious to others that he is not benefiting. He is suffering. This is because his body, and after long use, his mind, become poisoned by the substance. He may go on to use more and he may try to stop for a while, and may able to be able to do so. He may be going through a phase and can cease when he does not benefit from the experience. However, an addict will return to the substance unless he has a spiritual conversion and becomes involved in treatment. He gets incredible cravings! This is loss of control!

The dynamics are somewhat different in other aspects. Not even all addicts develop the same patterns and symptoms at the same pace or time. Some teens become totally out of control the first time they use. Others have an adaptation period that lasts for years whereas the using does not seem problematic. They can stop or use infrequently even only a couple of times a year but eventually return to addictive states and use worse than before. No matter how long or how frequent a person uses, the end result is the same. However, when untreated, all addicts look the same in the late stages and at death's door.

At some point thereafter he crosses the line to addiction, loss of control begins and tolerance builds and the addict uses more. The use may be slow enough that adaptation occurs slowly. This means that he learns to cover up the use and begins to cope by defending himself from the consequences by addictive thinking. Negative results and thus feelings then occur and the addict has to defend against these also. For example, shame takes over and the person begins to lower standards because of using, e.g., he may choose peers who are deep into addiction. This does not cause the using. This is a result, a symptom. It now can become apparent that the using must stop or very little change can occur. This is when you are losing your son more and more.

Shame and Redemption

Shame or remorse is a big issue in recovery. It keeps the addict from feeling good enough about self to be honest or to function with integrity. It also prevents him from building character and coming back from a relapse as he doesn't feel that he 'deserves' to get sober. He overcompensates with overconfidence and defiance. This can linger in recovery and must be 'countered' with constant contact with recovering people and eventual work with others who are trying to recover. This way the experiences that create the shame are put to good use by identifying and sharing with addicts new to recovery. This way, the negativity is neutralized. Otherwise, this shame can take the form of blaming others, minimizing the use, rationalizing, intellectualizing or justifying in any way he can imagine.

The addict has much difficulty seeing reality and develops delusional thinking. At this point, you have lost your son. This is not your son anymore. As above, this triggers all of the feelings of shock, terror, hurt, depression, anger and guilt in you, the parents. Remember parents, it is not your fault! Do not 'buy into' the problem. Again, do not react. Remember that you are going to intervene. You must wait until you can assert yourself during the intervention. Further, this problem is genetic. He did not ask for this problem and he did not cause it. Do not react. Be logical and then you can choose how you want to handle the situation.

Your other children, at least some of them, raised by the same parents are more than likely doing well, aren't they? Odds are that half of the male offspring will have this problem if it is on the male side of the family (Schuckitt, 1985). My point is that your son did not choose this problem. You, as parents, did not cause it with your parenting style. For the most part, genes caused it.

Denial

There is a language of denial. Much of the time, during his use, you'll see and hear diverting, evading, defocussing and other means of avoidance in order to change the subject from the topic of use. Along with this, you'll hear lies; the user cannot use and tell the truth about using to anyone except other users. This leads to association with a different peer group. Many times it will be mixed with others who do not use or are not addicted but, if addicted, your child eventually will choose the peer group who uses and are addicted. At this point you are losing your child to another family, a peer family of users. Do not react. Be logical. Denial is not a personal affront towards you.

The family can also get back into denial. Parents want their child to get well so badly that when they see improvement, they sometimes discontinue treatment in hope that he is now cured. At other times, the parents plan a trip for the family and take the child without prearrangement with treatment staff. This sends a message to the child that treatment can be usurped or undermined by the family. The goal is for the family to accept their powerlessness over this disease and to adapt to treatment protocol.

The Goal

As above, try not to blame, even when he or she 'tries' you. If you are going to Al-Anon, you will be much less likely to get into denial and you will therefore not 'act out' on your negative feelings. You will know that he does not intend to harm you. His rejection and betrayal are not personal. You will desensitize yourself from the initial shock and the inclination to either avoid the problem or explode that happens when a parent finds out that the child is using.

When the problem goes undetected and ignored, your child gets worse. The behavior gets worse. The defiance and betrayal, perhaps even stealing from the family or letting drug and/or alcohol users in your home who will steal your valuables, can get worse and be very provocative. Once more, this can lead to your feeling hurt, fearful and even enraged. The behaviors also trigger intense feelings of outrage and disbelief that your child can 'turn' on you even after you've devoted your life to him or her. This can occur especially after you've set boundaries for the first time and enforced them. Therefore, when you talk with him these feelings can leak out. You may even yell when discovering a new behavior or even explode in rage saying things that you regret at once. It is vital to let go of the rage and fear when you talk with him. A display of anger and careless words can sabotage the relationship.

If you have already exploded or said things that you regret you can repair this but be careful not to repeat the 'explosion'. You may also have a tendency to 'over-apologize'. Don't do it! Over-apologizing means that you take all of the responsibility for the problem. An addict will misinterpret or use this and surmise that all of the responsibility for the problem is yours. He may defocus from the real problem: his 'out-of-of control' drug and/or alcohol using, problems caused by his dependency, and inability to stop. As I have mentioned above, a child who is drug-affected will blame. If you apologize, they may blame the problem on you totally. Even if this has happened, I'm going to teach you how to avoid this when you have "the talk" (intervention) with him. For now, we'll focus on maintaining or repairing the relationship.

How to Cope

Again, do not avoid this problem. When we avoid the addiction, we are assisting the disease and the denial and avoidance comes back. In addition, if you are attending your twelve-step and family treatment meetings, you will have reasonable and realistic expectations regarding relapse and you won't be 'at your wit's end' if he doesn't stop.* You won't worry as much and won't be devastated if or when it happens. You'll be forewarned. You won't lash out at him. Remember, he is sick, not bad. A big part of him does not want this disease. We have to help him to recapture that part. This is the aim of this book – to help him find a way out of the darkness through a loving yet firm approach that 'holds the child accountable' for the consequences of his actions yet never allowing the problems to go unanswered.

Foundation in Counseling Relationship Theory

When I started taking counseling courses in the 1960's, Carl Rogers (1951) had completed his relationship focused theory on the core conditions of communication. I saw him in Houston, Texas in 1995 and he was still working on his beliefs and championing his cause of healthy communication. His facilitative conditions included warmth, empathy, respect, self-disclosure and congruence. These were the conditions that the counselor was responsible for establishing in the counseling session. These maximized the chance that the relationship would build by providing safety and trust, conditions that are ideal when communicating with and motivating your child. These same facilitative conditions can be the key to effective communication with your child. I encourage you to use them with your child. They form the cornerstone of healthy communication. Warmth is obvious. Empathy means walking in the other's shoes. Empathy is not sympathy. We do not pity the person or protect them. Whoever you protect you weaken. We must hold him accountable, help him grow, help him to think realistically. We simply understand that he is hurting. However, we expect growth just as a counselor expects growth. Expect stabilization, then continued growth. This is necessary in order to stay sober. Respect means that you don't talk down to him. Use "I" messages, e.g., "I feel hurt that you stole from me." State how you feel and think without analyzing, scolding, lecturing, advising or telling him anything. Set boundaries in a logical manner and not with anger, passive behavior or pity. Communication should not be fear-based. Be confident and speak from strength. Self-disclosure means that you can share how this problem has affected you. Again, "I" messages are important. This also motivates you to detach from the pain through an intervention. This means that you'll have to know what you are feeling and be able to communicate this. Otherwise, we fall into the trap of blame. Congruency means that you match your "insides with your outsides." You can say what you are feeling and not hold back. However, it does not mean that you 'let loose' with all of the negativity and yell at him. We'll talk later about assertiveness, saying what you mean but not in a mean way.

By the way, as above, you will slip. You will yell and criticize and blame and displace anger. Remember, you can repair the relationship. In fact, you can even make it better with an assertive yet sincere apology. This can be a good time to remind your child that you love him and this disease is tearing you up. The disease does hurt and angers all those in contact with it. Again, do not apologize for feeling distraught, angry, hurt, guilty or fearful. Apologize for the explosion or other behavior that you didn't like. Be confident and continue with your recovery. Do not act out of guilt. Do not buy that car for him!!!

I would like to elaborate on self-disclosure. Another person I have studied was Sid Jourard, a University of Florida professor who wrote The Transparent Self, a book in which he explained that the best way to get a person to open up and share is for you to do this. This gives the other a sense of safety and normalization. This also models openness. If your child has withdrawn, perhaps breaking connections with the family, teach him that, in order to communicate, we must talk and discuss our concerns and differences and position on his behavior. If he expresses his position, which is usually going to be strained, you can wait and then figure out how to manage this with your partner. This technique is very much a part of my counseling style with addicts and alcoholics.

Hold Him Accountable

These two concepts of facilitative conditions and openness/self-disclosure, along with Tough Love theory led me to develop my position on preservation/restoration of the relationship with an addictive child. Tough love means that you take charge of your home and be the leaders. Your child may have taken the family hostage, threatening to 'act out' if you confront him on his erratic or even abusive behavior. Do not let him do this. Protect your family. You are the parents. You are the leaders, the teachers, the breadwinners, the inspiration, the guides, the spiritual leaders. Lead! Your child, even if he is trying to continue to use and control the family, does not want this job. He is not qualified. He will live in fear if you step aside and let him and the disease take over. This will be expressed through an arrogant, overconfident attitude or through withdrawal. Do not let him sleep in, come and go as he wants, swear at family members, hang out with using peers, lie, cheat, steal, drop out of school, be truant or avoid homework. Hold him accountable by enforcing consequences every time. Be strong parents! Be a team!

Begin the Script Now

You can use all of these conditions, not be passive or aggressive and still get your point across. You can choose to be assertive. You can and need to be assertive, logical and firm. This is an art and must be studied and practiced. It occurs when you decide to act reasonably and not overly emotional because of the stress-related emotionality created by this disease. Now you can choose. Your main tool to learn is being a student yourself and learning the lesson, writing a script of the talk you are going to have with him, rehearsing the script, accepting feedback from a partner, and modifying the script to make it effective. It is vitally important to do this as suggested. I suggest that you follow this direction verbatim. Trust me you'll be able to influence your child if you follow my direction. I will cover this topic in more detail in chapter 9 but you can start now to write your script. Begin with your problems due to his using.

Cause

The psychological model of behavior states that thoughts trigger feelings that trigger behaviors. However, this does not work with addicts. The addict/alcoholic needs to stop thinking and trying to figure out the cause and take actions that are time-tested and true. Analyzing and intellectualizing the problem is the problem. The addict is an expert in bad thinking. He has a thinking disorder. He must act!

By this time you're probably 'getting this concept down' pretty well. All throughout this book I have and will be explaining accurate information/ thoughts on addiction that will help you to regulate your feelings that, in turn, will dictate your actions just as he must do. By now you have begun to look at this problem as a physiological illness that is not a matter of controlling or stopping the drug and/or alcohol use. Cravings are incredibly compelling and powerful. An addict usually does not have a chance of stopping or not stopping once they "cross the line" to addiction. This line occurs when will power ceases to exist and consequences no longer matter. They do not want this problem and do not know that it is progressive and always gets worse. This is a vital concern and needs to be addressed or all else gets worse. Intervene ASAP. It always gets worse.

Parenting

In my opinion, this problem has little to do with parenting and everything to do with parenting. Children who grow up with the same parents in the same house and are treated the same can turn out differently especially if one has the genetic predisposition for addiction and the other(s) does not. When a child who has a genetic predisposition for addiction drinks and/or uses drugs, he will eventually become addicted if he keeps using or may even cross the line at the first ingestion of a drink or a drug. This turns the child into someone you eventually do not recognize. This is not your fault!!! Again, let go of the guilt and see this problem as an illness. Be aware that your child does not want this disease either. Initially, it seduces him with good times and excitement and then "turns" on him, causing them to use poor judgment coupled with low inhibition. Your job is to know all of this, use it to think of him as having an illness, perhaps imagining him in a sickbed, and then taking action to help. This is where your parenting comes into play.

Not knowing the course of the disease, we can think they are choosing this, subsequently become angry at our powerless and their behavior, feel like a victim, see the behavior as willed and well thought out and, as stated before, proceed to 'act out' by yelling, blaming and overreacting. When we have studied this problem we can see that it has affected us tremendously, causing us to become emotionally distraught and maybe even enraged at the repeated and worsening threats, lies and series of betrayals. We need help also.* We have been deeply affected by the loss of our child. This is serious. We do not become rid of these feelings by merely thinking differently or wishing them away. Reinforcement of our realistic attitude is necessary, especially over time. We can get this reinforcement at an Al-Anon program.

Power Struggles

Now you can see how the relationship needs to be preserved because, when addiction is involved, the relationship can easily become destroyed or damaged. This disease has a 'life of its own' and can infiltrate a family and destroy it from within. Armed with accurate information and a new thought process about this problem, you can now feel compassion and confidence about taking actions that will be logical and helpful. Your behavior/intervention can now be based on empathy, warmth, respect, self-disclosure and congruency. In addition, you will be sure to influence him and avoid controlling or getting in a 'power struggle' with him. This is usually a 'lose-lose' situation. You want a 'win-win.' We don't have to be right. We simply assert ourselves as the parents and enforce reasonable consequences. Use a confident and loving approach. After all, you wouldn't judge him if he had diabetes.

If you saw a car crash into a pole you may think that the person was drunk. What would your immediate attitude be? I saw this happen in a parking lot one Saturday morning and automatically thought that the person was wrong and of danger to others, a nuisance. As it turned out, the person was diabetic and was almost passed out. My attitude changed to empathy automatically. I never once thought that he should have never gone into a coma and should have snapped out of it. The irony was that I was at a radio station doing a show on addiction.

This is simply another type of disease. We have to try not to judge the person even with evidence of behaviors that seem very illogical. Therefore, have a firm attitude that he can respect and without judgment. In addition, do not need his approval yet be caring and warm. Gain respect - do not give in. Take charge of your family!

If you remember one thing from this chapter, remember that this problem is treatable. Embrace your relationship with him with caring firmness. You must next know for sure what you are treating.

CHAPTER EIGHT

LOOK AND IDENTIFY - STEP 3

You have to know the problem before you can work on the solution.
Joe M.

In this chapter I'm going to tell you the biggest mistake that is made in the field of recovery. It is one that keeps addicts and alcoholics drunk and high, skews research results and accounts for the deaths of many addicts and alcoholics.

Misdiagnoses

We have covered recognizing the problem and embracing the relationship. We are now going to look at the problem specifically. As far as I'm concerned, the biggest mistake made in the treatment of addiction is misdiagnoses. Many addicts are diagnosed as depressed, a mental health diagnosis. Well, since the late 60's, I have never met a happy, truly happy, detoxifying addict. This is simply illogical. Emile Durkheim (1898) questioned whether addiction was slow suicide. If a person is committing slow suicide, he has to be unhappy and spiritually bankrupt. One can't be slowly killing oneself, consciously or unconsciously, without feeling sad and depressed. The words contented or happy alcoholic or addict does not go together. We've known this for centuries.

Before you can work on a solution you need to know the problem. Without this knowledge, you may treat a secondary problem or the wrong problem. For example, if you operate on an alcoholic's ulcer and remove part of the stomach, the ulcer will return if the person returns to drinking. The ulcer returns worse than ever. If we help a depressed alcoholic with his depression and he keeps ingesting a depressant (alcohol), we are not treating the primary problem. We are treating symptoms. We are treating depression, a natural consequence of drinking but not the cause of the problems. We must determine the primary problem. Then we can treat the problem. Otherwise, we will treat a symptom and the problem will worsen. Therefore, we need to know what the problem is.

Further, some alcoholics get labeled manic depressive. While about 3% to 4% of any population is mentally ill, I believe that this diagnosis is rare with alcoholics. In addition, I believe that many addicts and alcoholics are over medicated for many misdiagnoses. Many die from over-medication because these medications are causing the problem. I have seen this time after time for many years by well-meaning doctors. I recently attended a conference and heard the former president of ASAM, Dr. Michael Miller; state that Medical Doctors (M.D.s) do not get much information on addiction. Their coursework is very limited. New coursework in addictionology is improving on this but we have a long way to go. Age-old stereotypes have to be broken.

For example, experience can form stereotypes. When I worked in an emergency room back in the seventies, end-stage alcoholics would be brought in to be 'lavaged' after overdosing. The attitude of the staff toward them was negative. The alcoholic was not greeted with any sense of warmth usually due to his sense of drama, excitability or seemingly apathy or difficulty in taking care of self. Both extremes were turnoffs. At times, the same person would come in due to self-imposed illness or tragic behavior or consequences. This gives the impression that, "He's just drunk again." "Oh no, it's that drunk, Johnny. He's going to take all of our time again. He should just stop drinking. I've got better things to do than tend to a drunk who isn't helping himself." These attitudes come honestly. The drunken alcoholic who is inconsiderate, self-centered and imposing on a busy staff is not a very likable guest in their emergency room. This is understandable yet inaccurately judged due to a lack of understanding of the disease. This reinforces the already existing stigma of alcoholism.

When approaching this issue from a training point of view, M.D.s is actually handicapped by a lack of information about addiction. Their intent is to help but the damage that misdiagnoses and multi-prescription drugs do is incredible. M.D.s is medical doctors who prescribe medicine. This is their training. The problem is that oftentimes medicine is the problem. Many addicts look for M.D.s who will prescribe medicine that is addicting or that they can sell to get money in order to buy their drug of choice. This has happened in Florida during the past 10-15 years with opiates. People came from all over the USA to purchase medicine from pain clinics because they could. The problem was that there was no way to track the sale of these medications and many people would obtain pain meds for simply showing an MRI, suggesting a back problem, to a clinic that prescribed opiates. Drug dealers would force their 'clients' to use prescriptions to buy drugs for them. The clinics dispensed the drugs freely. This is now being addressed and kids are changing to less expensive heroin.

When referring an addict to a medical doctor, it is important to use an M.D. who understands addiction. I mean use one who understands that the cravings trigger a disease that is a death sentence. Addiction leads to death, one problem at a time. When there are no 'felt consequences' and, in fact, are rewards, especially medicine, the addict/alcoholic will think that they are right in using because the M.D. (M.D.s have expert power) gave them permission, recommended these drugs. Some addicts interpret being given a drug prescription as 'permission' to abuse the drug because it was prescribed. M.D.s need to know about the disease concept (Ohlms, 1991) and how cravings for alcohol are about twenty times more powerful than morphine cravings. These, when triggered, are very powerful and almost impossible to resist without a "Program" and, at times, medication. The addict, unless in strong, strong, quality recovery uses, cannot stop and progressively goes downward.

I had a friend who claimed to be in recovery, would celebrate his sobriety anniversary every year and not be able to stand straight because he was so high. When he saw me, he would say that his prescriptions were given by an M.D. I hadn't asked him about the medications. He would offer the information. I think he was feeling guilty but couldn't talk about it overtly because he was so incredibly drug-affected that he wasn't very coherent. He would complain of incredible back pain, use a cane for walking, but could shoot pool for hours without the cane and without complaining. This self-deception is a defect of the addict. It is a defense against the truth. When the truth is known and the person wants to keep using there is internal conflict. This is psychic pain and the addict abhors pain.

The solution would be for doctors to consult with an expert on addiction before prescribing and then talk with their patient about the need for monitoring. This means contracting for the addict to attend and participate in twelve-step meetings, attend outpatient treatment, have their parent or spouse hold the medication, dispense it according to plan and have the patient report for weekly follow-up in addition to talking to someone daily about the possibility of cravings. Misdiagnoses are prevalent in our world. So is addiction mistreatment. The addict needs to learn the tools and make recovery connections needed in order to maintain recovery.

Further, many of our elderly have this genetic predisposition to addiction, are prescribed medication as they get older and become addicted instantly. Or, having triggered the problem early in life and aware of the consequences, abstain for decades only to re-trigger the problem when they are appropriately prescribed medication later on in life. They nor the medical community have no clue that they are now in late stages of addiction. The effects of the drugs on the body are quick, tragic and lethal. This phenomenon is called progression. The problem always gets worse, never better. Using gets worse over time. An addict can stop using for years and years, relapse, and return to where he left off plus all of the time that he was abstinent. In other words, it appears as though the addict's disease has progressed even though he hasn't used for years. This progression does not seem to be the same for all addicts or alcoholics, once again signaling us to the treacherous nature of the problem. This disease is the dark side. It cripples and then kills. The solution is the light side or Sunlight of the Spirit.

Family Bias

Furthermore, as mentioned earlier, no one wants this problem in the family. This is another reason or excuse for the family to avoid the problem or fail to see it accurately. Family members may think that, "this is a problem other people have." Sometimes we find depression or bipolar or borderline or schizoid affective or adjustment disorder with depressive features diagnoses to be much more palatable than alcoholism. Most addicts want to have anything other than addiction. There is still a stigma on addiction. That is one of the main reasons that it is still pandemic. The problem remains 'behind closed doors' because of the family's resistance to treatment. They suffer from the same disease, only their mindset is that they are the solution and do not need meetings or to focus on themselves. This leads to lack of accurate diagnosis.

Stigma of the Disease

Continuing, who wants to be an alcoholic? I have heard dozens of people say that they wanted to be mentally ill instead of alcoholic because they didn't want to be alcoholic. Most everyone born up to this time in history thinks of an alcoholic/addict as someone who is unemployable, deplorable, at late stages and chronic; in others words, disgusting. They avoid it. The stigma keeps the alcoholic and/or addict from getting sober also. The addict will try to convince you that the problem is a phase, social or a minimal problem. This is not logical. If this were true, then it should be easy to stop.

The Course of Treatment

Addicts and alcoholics do not get sober by analyzing the cause of the addiction. This does not help. Many addicts get sober and, because of a need to control the disease and the use, try to figure it out. It's almost as though they believe that they can handle it, drink safely, if they can figure it out. This does not work because no one has addiction figured out. Once more, the addict must take action after giving up the desire to make sense of it all. The addict must focus on the solution, the spiritual conversion that was given us freely and thrives in our twelve-step programs. Lost and hopeless souls are restored to sanity and the cravings neutralized after entering this healing process. The co-addict must take the same path.

Stages of Addiction

What is true is that addiction is not a choice yet it is a choice. At first, the alcoholic may have freedom to drink or not to drink depending on the type of alcoholic he is but later on in the progression he is compelled to indulge in a manner that shocks and/or disgusts most normal people. This is difficult to understand unless you have been there. However, who would consciously choose to spiral downward? The truth is that there is a physiological component to addiction and that there are stages of addiction. What we notice in the media and in our personal lives are people in late stages of addiction. This is because it is noticeable. We form our opinion of addiction based on this second hand experience when we should base our judgment on valid and reliable research, multiple experiences or years of experience with the disease. This can interfere with an accurate diagnosis as we can still tend to minimize the problem and its symptoms.

We do not notice early stages of addiction because, in early stages, the symptoms are usually not as grave as the second or third stages of addiction. In early stage addiction, there is sometimes an adaptation period that can last for about a decade. During this stage, the disease is hardly noticeable in many cases. In the middle stage, which is difficult to define chronologically, the consequences are more noticeable but may manifest in low to moderate problems and not be blatantly noticeable at this point either. They can also be managed by well meaning enablers and subsequently covered up. Further, when we do not want to see this problem, it is easier for a co-addict to ignore or mistake it for another problem. We do not want to see the problem because it is inconvenient and uninvited. We may also think that recognition means that we have to risk a confrontation with the addict, risk threatening his 'treasured' drug and lifestyle. The therapist or anyone in the helping field risks losing his client. We may also risk losing a relationship with a father, a spouse or another loved one. Sometimes when the addict is the breadwinner, we risk losing an income or a pension and have to trust God that we will survive without the addict. When the addict is our child, we risk losing the worst loss imaginable – the loss of our child.

The Adult Child of an Alcoholic (ACOA) or the co-dependent does not see the problem because I believe that the anxiety created by the disease in the family keeps him from knowing the truth or seeing the obvious. In addition, there is a family agreement that it's to be kept secret. The chaos in the home created by the disease keeps the family on edge, never knowing the danger of the confusion. This can be true even when the addict gets drunk in front of everyone at the dinner table.

These are some of the reasons that this problem still exists even though we may detect it early. The addict/alcoholic may never identify the disease in any stage. He is usually in denial. He cannot tell the truth about his disease because he does not know the truth. You can connect an addict/alcoholic in denial to a polygraph machine and the machine (addict/alcoholic) will register true as he tells you that he does not have a problem with addiction. He does not know and cannot know until he is told by someone who cares (at the same time as consequences occur) and tells him in a very powerful way. My intent is to explain how you and your family can do this. He needs us to intervene!

Cigarettes have been exposed as lethal as has poor diet as has poor exercise habits. However, we have turned these problems around. Still, we somehow do not recognize drug and alcohol addiction. Comedians joke about it. They drink and are high on stage and in public while entertaining us. We laugh at them and thus reinforce the problem. Movie stars smoke 'wacky weed' and make preposterous remarks while 'loaded' and we look up to them. Athletes get drunken driving charges and we send them to schools to tell our children not to get drunken driving charges. Politicians get drunk and high and hire prostitutes on our money and we ignore this. And the 'beat goes on; the disease carries on and on and on and on...' We need you to help!

How do we diagnose accurately? Well, we really shouldn't. Trained treatment professionals should. However, we can easily tell if a child is in a stage of experimentation or social use or abuse. Sometimes it is obvious to tell because the symptoms are so progressed that there's no doubt. Other times, the problem is subtle or enablers prevail and absorb the disease. On most other occasions, the co-dependents shield or insulate the addict by paying the fine, getting the lawyer, putting up bail money or just co-signing the belief system ("I'm different", "I'm smarter", "I'm, I'm, I'm"...). There are many ways to enable. All addicts have enablers.

When the enablers detach/leave, the addict cannot use anymore. The 'bottom line' is that it doesn't matter how much or how often one uses. What matters is what happens when a person uses. If a person drinks and/or drugs and wants more, has repeated consequences and withdrawal symptoms and continues to use - that is addiction. You can see this now. He cannot. He needs us to intervene!

Scott G

CHAPTER NINE

ALTERNATIVES: STRATEGIZE AND REHEARSE - STEP 4

He who fails to plan is planning to fail.
Winston Churchill

The strategy that you implement will depend upon three factors. One is the relationship that you have with God and yourself; second is the relationship that you have with your child; third is the relationship that you have with your spouse or significant other and your team.

The relationship with God has to do with priorities. The alcoholic/addict is searching for something when he gets high. He is escaping from this world to a higher world. In order to get sober and clean he must seek a Higher Entity that is positive and not destructive. He must have a spiritual conversion. He has to turn from the hedonistic self-destruction to a belief in a Power greater than him. The twelve-step concept of God is very, very liberal. The idea I have gleaned from readings, a religious upbringing, and sober teachings is to stop worshiping alcohol, drugs, self and other addictions and turn toward a Creative Intelligence or whatever conceptualization the individual has of God.

The relationship that you have with your child is important because this will help you to determine your course of action. If your child's use is advanced, the relationship may be much distanced. You may have to go back to step two and work on this. If he is still your dependent and you still have a decent relationship, you have 'leverage' and can operate as a caring parent and still plan to intervene in his best interests. If he is more independent yet cooperative, you may still have leverage if he still listens to you. The relationship, if distant, may rely heavily upon another person's involvement which he trusts and respects. This may be someone who you have to bring into the plan provided they are clean and sober, stable, cooperative and motivated to help. Whatever the relation status, you can plan a strategy that is effective. Parents who have faith and trust in God in the same way can effectively influence their child.

When the child is close to you and not too 'far gone' with his drug and or alcohol use, the chances are better that he will listen to you. There is still a chance that he can be educated. At this point, your stability is crucial to his success. Being affected emotionally and psychologically by stable, non-addicted parents who attend Al-Anon can be the key to his recovery. However, planning is still crucial.

The Team

The third part of your strategy is to have a good relationship with your partner and team. The first and most vital part of teamwork is to unite with your team and talk, write, and develop a script that you will use when you intervene. The number one guideline for the team is that everyone who is part of this team must be stable. If anyone is drinking or using, emotionally 'flooded,' i.e., emotionally distraught, dramatic and too angry or sad or fearful or guilt-ridden to be logical and caring but firm, they must be eliminated from the team unless they can quickly 'work through' this issue to resolution. When performing an intervention, there cannot be any participant who speaks from an angry or guilty position, either pushing the person away or giving the addict the impression that they will not hold him accountable. An addict will manipulate people because he wants to continue using and will sense weakness and exploit it by trying to buy time, blame or negotiate his way out of the actions that you want him to take.

The second team guideline is to stick to your guns. Do not attempt to negotiate non-negotiable rules. Even when you say these are non-negotiable, he may try to negotiate. This process can be unconscious and even the addict cannot see his motives much of the time. With committed members educated about substance abuse on the team, his negotiating tactics will not be honored. A good response to use when he tries to 'test' you with pleas is, "This is not a debate." or "This is not debatable."

The parents must lead the way. You are the decision makers. However, if you are going to influence him by means of an intervention, you must again let go of the need to control as parents and teach this to your team. Again,

I like the word influence because it means that you have his best interests at heart. He will know this if it is presented well. Persuasion or control will dissuade him from working with you. He will sense your need to control and use this to blame you and leave.

Your intent is important. Intend to help and do what is best for your child. This can be difficult. Realize that you may still not know what is best. If you have not sought out a coach or therapist, this may be the time to do so. An objective 'coach' is vital at this step. You need someone who can be objective especially if you still may want to protect him. I suggest you use a trained therapist, trained in addiction intervention. The money is well spent. The disease, with its negative consequences will cost a fortune. Pay for treatment, not tragedies. The sooner you make this final commitment the better chances you create for his and the family's success.

The Parenting Team

Usually the team consists of the parents and perhaps a child or an aunt, uncle or other relative. It may include a friend who cares about your son and has seen his behavior outside of the home. This can be very valuable. Once you have gathered this group of helpers, you must balance the parental approach.

As before, the parents usually are different in two respects. One will be too lenient and the other too stern. On the other hand, when there is agreement, you are a "step ahead." If not, the ideal approach must be negotiated. There must be agreement on parenting. There is a middle ground upon which you must agree. This being the case, the parents must communicate and agree to negotiate their differences. If there is an unspoken disagreement, this must be brought into the open and negotiated. Negotiation is important for interventions because it allows fairness and cohesion in the relationship. This negotiation may involve two or three counseling sessions. During the course of therapy, both must write their script and allow the other to comment on it.

Further, each must write scripts and work at their delivery until they have balanced the extremes and agreed on a unified approach based on caring firmness. Then and only then can communication be delivered as a team. Rehearsal is vital so that there can be feedback and remediation. The script needs to be read fluently and without fear, anger, pity, sadness or judgment. There must be a presence of confidence yet not overconfidence. Caring and firmness need to be shown with equal strength yet without force.

As mentioned before, one way to sabotage this plan is to involve someone who has a problem with drugs or alcohol. Here a word of caution is in order: If you have a drug and/or alcohol user present, your child will immediately begin to see the meeting as weak and will not cooperate. If you have to wonder whether any one person besides the child should be there because of his or her using, eliminate them at once. You have your answer. A manipulating addict will use this to strengthen denial and project blame on the family and especially this person. This is understandable. Anyone who is not willing to abstain from alcohol and drugs has a concern with alcohol and drugs. There is a relationship that is important to them. You may in fact end up helping two people.

The team meeting can take place when the parents have met, agreed on a balanced and unified approach whereas they back each other up, agree on the team members and have asked all to join. The team members can then be contacted, trained in the same manner as you and then a meeting time and place for the intervention agreed upon. Sometimes this involves bringing someone in from out of town. An uncle, aunt, grandfather or friend can be immensely helpful and create a sense of urgency about the meeting when they have traveled to attend this critical intervention.

Specifics – The Script

If you are seeing a therapist, and, again, I recommend getting an expert, let him or her take charge of the direction and planning. If not, train your team. Have them write a script they will present during the intervention. Begin your meeting cordially and explain briefly that 'we're here to try to save a life.' This involves everyone agreeing to a balanced approach, writing, rehearsing and delivering a script. The main guideline is to promote effective communication and eliminate lecturing or interrupting and be brief, the less the better (three to ten minutes). Follow the lead of the facilitator (a therapist or a parent).

The written script will be in three parts. The first stating, in each participant's own words, that they care about your child. Second, a brief description of an event when he was drinking or using when you had strong feelings of fear, anger, hurt or guilt about the incident and thought of it for days after it occurred. Third, include a treatment entry stipulation that must be met. For example, "I want you to go to treatment today. We have your bags packed and have them in the car, have contacted a treatment center and have the admission process completed." All usually agree on treatment of some sort. This may also be outpatient with daily twelve-step attendance and setting the home up as a therapeutic environment, intensive outpatient, i.e., three to six hours daily for three to five days weekly or a recovery group or groups with a combination of individual, family or marital therapy.

Other boundaries that you can establish may include, in your own words, no contact, placement for him if he is active, estrangement, separation from him, or any consequence you are willing to enforce. Do not include any consequences that you will not enforce. Think through this carefully. Remember, you are creating the leverage and must be willing to enforce this. You are doing this because consequences can stop the addiction. This may be 'new' but it is true love. You love your child enough to make sure they do not 'give in' to this disease anymore. If you set a consequence now, he will not have to keep using and have twice the consequence next year.* If you give in and do not enforce the consequence, this will strengthen the belief system that he can control the people around them and he will feel very powerful against any consequence, again thinking that he can 'beat the game' and continue to use. He will think that he can override this attempt to stop him and is therefore smarter than others, can continue to use and will be indignant towards anyone trying to take away his using. This is how an addict thinks in this situation. It is based on feelings of self-importance and omnipotence that are drug-induced. This is what an addict thinks. He will then require much more of a tragedy to wake him up. Read on for a personal example.

Personal Anecdote

I was responsible for a DUI in 1975 in Denver, Colorado. I was guilty and should have received more consequences than I did. I thought I had gotten lucky but, after I got sober and clean, I realized I was wrong. I didn't get lucky. I got unlucky. I received an overnight stay in a detoxification center. I was taken to jail, and then transferred to a detox center overnight, where I woke up half-drunk and hung over, detoxifying as I painfully walked to the front desk, the longest walk of my life. When asked, "when was the last time you were here," I became indignant (ego-driven) like any addict, asked to see the supervisor, met in a private room, and explained to her how to do an intake. She either bought my 'prideful attitude' or just wanted to get rid of me and said she would "look into this, do better training" and then discharged me. This important therapist from New York left, walked home, feeling completely depressed and saddened down deep, but intoxicated by the so-called "victory" and got drunk that night. I had showed them. While this story is kind of humorous on the surface, it is tragically serious 'down deep.' I paid $250 for a judge to release me, had no significant consequences, thought that the incident was due to me celebrating too much as I had beaten a major pool player, a world champ, and had overindulged because I was celebrating. Reality was that I had gotten drunk on a regular basis for the past fifteen years. It was this thinking, my best thinking, which got me a chair at a twelve-step meeting.

I continued to drink until 1986 and developed Barrett's Esophagus, a triglyceride count over 2000, chronic fatigue syndrome, a poor immune system, emphysema, ruined relationships, a poor character, guilt and remorse, hopelessness, apathy, paranoia, suicide ideation and depression. I can name about 100 more consequences but I think you get the picture. I was very unlucky that night. This is what I gleaned from that experience at about six months without a drug or drink. It took that long to 'come to my senses' about that and many other problems like that incident.

Over the years, two girlfriends told me they were concerned about my drinking but I dismissed their information because they too were using. On another occasion, I woke up with two girls on the living room floor with beer bottles all around me, empty bottles. They were shooting heroin and told me they were concerned that I had a drinking problem. My thinking was that I needed to get as far away from them as possible. By the way, that is still my thinking about those two. However, this strengthened my denial system and I continued to think that my problem was different, minimal compared to theirs or most any other addict. I was, and always will be, the type of addict who drank beer, bud light, smoked pot and had used cocaine maybe five times, used Tylenol 3's maybe ten times, hash oil at times, pot laced with substances of which I was not aware, hallucinogens twice and I'm not sure but I think that's the extent of my use.

I had an intense dislike for 'hardcore addicts' who were antisocial personalities. I used this to build a case that defended my addiction and could see addiction only as something I saw as completely estranged from and disgusting to me. I thought that I looked good compared to them. I didn't know this to be true until I just wrote it. I guess we "learn as we go." I always had someone with whom I could compare my use and build a case where their use was much, much worse but I never knew I used this thinking as a defense against the truth. All in all, the "two girls" was not a good intervention. This was no way to do an intervention.

My consequences looked exponentially more serious when I began to attend twelve-step meetings. Only then could I begin to see that I had been spared an alcoholic/addict death. I had been given a gift of recovery that I can never pay back. However, it's a joy to try. I got better over the last twenty-five years. I seemed to be easier to get along with; life got better. People also seemed to get better to get along with also. AS I GOT BETTER, EVERYTHING ELSE GOT BETTER. I have seen hundreds of alcoholics and addicts get better this way. I really have. My deepest desire is that you can join me and millions of others who have been spared a life worse than death.

Commitment

Moving along, by the end of the intervention, your child has to know that you love him, have been deeply affected by his using and are not going to let this go. He must see you are stable, that you do not use alcohol to excess (check with your partner on this) and do not abuse drugs. You are healthy and committed to his change. You are not going to live with this problem anymore. It is destroying your family.

Your child must also realize and feel that this is a cooperative effort to help and not a conspiracy to control him because you are trying to overpower him. He won't be overpowered for long if at all. He does not have to get sober and clean. Nonverbal language, head nods and gestures will let him know that you support each other but are not against him. Help him join with you. However, remember that your child is drug/alcohol affected. This means that there is warped thinking. The way he interprets what you say will be motivated by a desire to control. Again, the alcoholic/addict tends to try and blame someone else for the problem, rationalizing his behavior, and thus prove he is right. Remember that he is thinking with a mind that has been altered. His brain desires and chooses the drug. His thoughts are usually extremely self-centered and hell-bent on being free and hedonistic. His best friend, drugs and alcohol, are being threatened and he will fight to the end unless you give him "an offer he can't refuse." You have to win him over with love, a caring attitude, and a genuine concern for his safety and success. I know that you, as parents, have this love. It is your job to let him know that you still care for him. He may not feel worthy and may think everyone is sick and tired of him just as he is. Let him know that you haven't given up on him.

Use the following approach. Do not argue the point. Simply be aware that an addict's thinking is regressed and this is dependent on genetics, duration and frequency of use. Do not believe what he says. Believe what you see. Again, if there are problems caused by the use and there is continued use, you usually have addiction. The disease is characterized by continued use in the presence of adverse consequences (ASAM, 2011, AMA, 1956, AA, 1938).

The following script incorporates the three part model that I suggest using:

TABLE 8 - THE SCRIPT

This 'offer' can be done with preparation and unification of the team and a well rehearsed intervention that is:

(1) Direct, yet caring,

(2) With a specific explanation of the problem behavior and your feelings,

(3) A consequence for noncompliance and a request for treatment.

This is the intervention strategy. More specifically, you could say:

(1) "We love you." or "We still care." or "You're my son and I love you."

(2) "This problem, your using has upset our home" or "When you fell on the stairs Friday" or "I feel angry that you have stolen money from us" or "I feel afraid for your life because you are driving when intoxicated" or "You owe money to a drug dealer and I feel disgraced and angry and afraid" or "I feel sad that you're not able to quit. "

(3) "Because of this 'out of control' behavior, I have to, 'Ask you to leave,' or 'Ask you to go to inpatient treatment,' 'Insist that you not use in our house,' 'Call the police,' or 'End our relationship until you go to treatment.'"

Butkins © 2012

The above is an example of a script that you can use as a template for your intervention. Each member writes out their personalized specific script based on his experience and feelings toward the addict. You can elaborate somewhat but I encourage you to be brief and concise. The consequences need to be strong enough so that you can detach. Try to think of your peace of mind as being the goal and design the script so that you can stop your preoccupation with him. At this point, I hope you can see that attempts to help have not helped. They have unintentionally contributed to the problem. Detaching now is your child's best chance to enter recovery. Try to understand my intent by understanding my meaning. I want you to keep your relationship with your child loving and keep your love and bond with him. Do not detach from your love for him or your loyalty or dedication for him. Give him his greatest gift by detaching from reinforcement/reward for his self-destructive behaviors that will end in his death. If you try to take care of this for him he will not have to take the action necessary for him to recover. When you hold him accountable for his actions and reward him for positive efforts, he will succeed in recovery. We have to motivate him to want to recover. Any attempt at doing it for him will prevent him from arriving at this place of surrender.

He will test you. Be prepared for this and commit to your position.

When you have written down your intervention script, rehearse it with your spouse. Be sure you read your child accurately and are not simply enabling and being easy on him because you do not want to upset the applecart. Make sure you have specific behaviors to point out. Use these for the intervention script. Vagueness gives him wiggle room so be specific. Vague references to behaviors allow argument. In addition, do not let him divert. Keep the communication focused.

Remember that treatment will not cure your child. The child's behaviors get better in recovery but he never becomes perfect. When he uses, many families get so sick of the problem that they give up without realizing it, without saying it. At first, they begin to help with efforts to protect and then enable. This progresses to rejection and rage and ends in efforts to control the child's behavior and eventually the child.* This is not the addict's responsibility. It is always the co-addict's responsibility to learn and consistently practice self-control over his or her emotions.* This discipline is possible with Al-Anon and/or therapy.

Do not give up. Stay close to your team and encourage them while they encourage you. As above, let go of any desire to fix him, to force him to quit. This approach will backfire. Again, addicts hate to be forced or told what to do. Let go and adhere to a plan. Commit to take care of yourself and the family. Commit to this plan and follow through. When you see that this problem is treacherous and will kill, you can commit much more easily. View it as a fatal illness because it is. Commit to getting your child into treatment just as you would if he had cancer or diabetes and was in denial. It can work if you follow directions. The hardest part, the newest part for parents, is to see this as fatal and follow up with a well-planned and well-intended intervention. "Old habits die hard" and the need to give up control to experts is difficult because this is so grave.

However, I have seen recovering parents who attend twelve-step Programs or are very united and strong keep their child at home without other treatment and eventually get the child help due to helping him out of denial by enforcing consequences. These were parents who would not let one aberrant behavior go without consequences. When the child relapsed, they would enforce their home contract. Since they never damaged the sense of caring yet instilled confidence in their parenting by being firm and 'sure' of themselves, the child could trust their judgment. Family rules of abstinence, curfew, school and structure were upheld consistently.

If you do the same and get treatment for the family (Al-Anon), you will see success. If you revert to treating this yourself, you will probably not succeed. Lastly, efforts to get him to treatment depend on what your relationship with him is and what you've tried. Sometimes you have to detach but at times telling him firmly to 'just go' (strong parenting) can work, especially when he is very ambivalent.

CHAPTER TEN

INTERVENTION - STEP 5

The ancestor of every action is a thought.
Ralph Waldo Emerson

You have written your script and rehearsed. Hopefully, you have addressed the weak parts of it and have polished it with the help of others. You must use "I" messages when speaking of your feelings, have specific, not vague, examples of your vignettes and then have measurable consequences.

TABLE 9 - EXAMPLE OF SCRIPT

For example, say, "I really love you and am fearful. The reason for my concern is that you are driving while intoxicated. Because of this, you haven't earned the privilege of using the car until you have entered treatment and remain there for three months, are drug and alcohol free, in recovery as seen and reported by qualified treatment staff and have earned it back," instead of, "You have messed up and I'm taking the car until you do better."

Butkins © 2012

Once you have rehearsed this, you will be able to say your part meaningfully and effectively. Now you can present your script. Your facilitator is prepared with a format and you have made arrangements for the meeting. It is best to let your child know that you are having a family meeting and that he needs to be there. Integrity is paramount so don't trick him. If you have trouble getting him to the meeting, this is a family control problem and must be addressed. No matter what has happened in the past, decide to take charge of your family. This is a time when we must control the entire event. Remember, there is a part of him that wants out. How we do this is not through force but with parental power. This is your family. Take charge. Remember, children do not want this disease, do not want to regress like they have and, again, do not want to be in charge of the family. They want you to take charge, the sooner the better. Two united parents who back each other are stable and are hard to defy. A team can have a similar impact. They agree on the direction of the intervention and the actions they are taking and support each other. Again, your child wants help. He wants you to take charge. It is scary to take charge of a family when you are young, have a limited education, limited contacts, little job or life experience and no way to support a family. Set the precedent. When you do this in a strong manner, you avert the strength and duration of later 'testing' that is inevitable. You are setting the precedent for further negotiating. You are setting the boundaries. "When the enablers leave, the user cannot use."

The Beginning:

Once you're in the room you, as parents, or a therapist have to state that you're here because all of you are concerned about his drug and/or drug use and want to talk with him. State that you are worried for him and that you are all going to say what you have to say to him and that you want him to hear everyone out. Then he will have his turn to talk.

As mentioned before in this reading, your child has built a defense system to guard against the pain of his disease (the 'bottom' or consequences). This serves to allow the person to continue use of the drugs and alcohol. The defense system consists of a mindset, a belief system, formed of many thoughts or beliefs that all point toward one thought that states, "It's ok to drink or drug." This system of justification has many parts, many thoughts that make up a belief system that is delusional or out of touch with reality, insane. Even though there are periods of lucidity/clarity and coherent thought, this delusion that "it's ok to kill myself because I'm doing it slowly" or "it's not that bad" will prevail all throughout the intervention. It is this thinking that has to be challenged and overcome. This cannot be done by force, controlling or lecturing. Remember, do not lecture. You will offend his sense of pride. Logic usually doesn't work and will only serve to trigger the intellectualization of the child, the debater in him, and the defiant side of him. This is how he thinks. Many times his thinking will be based on this defiance and misplaced, subconscious, fragmented resentments and fears that he cannot separate from your efforts to help him. You can easily become the enemy if you try too hard. The goal is to get him to cooperate. However, when you share what you're feeling, you can connect. This is a non-aggressive approach that usually invites cooperation instead of defiance. It's difficult to argue with feelings.

Intervening:

Performing an intervention is quite a task. You are attempting to change an addict's mind when they cannot see why they should think differently. Hopefully, you now can see what you're up against. First, it takes love to get through the wall of denial. Denial has its own set of thoughts. Cravings are generated by these thoughts of denial and may be only the life force your child has right now. It becomes second-nature for him to think this way. Next, relate your concerns to him (due to the consequences of his addiction), specifying feelings of fear, anger, sadness, and/or guilt. Present your report as someone who has been harmed by his behavior yet avoid voice inflections or looks that insinuate judgment. Your rendition must be presented in a way that's not only palatable but completely believable and acceptable so that these vignettes replace his impaired thinking. What we are attempting to circumvent are the addict's self-deception, easily generated feelings of rage and blame, self-indulgent terror and complete lack of concern for others. It takes his "loved ones" to present this in a sophisticated manner so as to break through the denial. This can be the start of his spiritual journey. Love conquers all!

As outlined above, deliver the first two parts of the script and pay special attention that you end with clear consequences (part three). Make sure that you have rehearsed your consequences – detailing exactly what you will do or not do as a result of his possible refusal to get help. If he does agree to treatment, follow through with a pre-determined treatment center and with arrangements for treatment entry made, transportation and clothing provided and payment obligations made. If he does not agree, if he wants to wait, enforce the consequences – detach! Simply let him know that you can't support him anymore as long as he refuses treatment and that you will help him when he sincerely asks for help. Remember, do not explode at him. He will use this to blame you. Now end the intervention with love. Do not engage and do not debate!!!

It is important that you do your best to deliver the best intervention that you can. Rehearse it well, accept any feedback from an expert therapist and deliver it with caring conviction. By doing so, you are either helping him to 'break denial' or you are planting seeds that can grow if he remembers your words with fond memories.

Your child will test your rules when he begins to crave his drug of choice

Your efforts will make a difference

Lay a Strong Family Direction

Beware that there is usually a 'return to use' called relapse that occurs within the first three months of recovery. If they know that the leverage, you, is intact and unbending, there is more of a tendency to stay sober and clean. This attitude starts here with the intervention. It is here where we begin to set the stage for recovery – yours and his. Your attitude of caring yet unwillingness to tolerate his self-destructive tendencies will begin this journey only if you are firm and transmit this to him at this time. Hopefully, this 'buys time' for him to clear up his confused mind and see that the real leverage is life itself. Then, the child has an opportunity to stay clean for this reason and the motivation becomes internalized. He is doing this for himself. Thus, he is self-motivated. This is the ultimate goal. We want him to want to go to his twelve-step meetings, develop spiritually, then mentally and emotionally and physically, become devoted to family, obtain a job and/or education and become a respected member of society. These should happen in exactly this order. Recovery and meetings must come first. Anything different will result in the new priority being lost, perhaps forever. As a focal point of this chapter, this ongoing action is the cornerstone of an ongoing, stable recovery that lasts. Knowledge must be transformed into action. When the recovering person goes to meetings, he sees the people who quit going to meetings come back after a relapse and show and explain how awful it still is out there. This and helping others is probably the only motivation that works over time.

Remember, the cravings are temporarily arrested and can return by ingesting any mood-altering chemical that can be triggered by going back to the old neighborhood, hanging around with old friends who use, watching TV where someone is using or any personal reminder of the feeling of euphoria. This is called "euphoric recall" and it is deadly.

Sometimes the first attempt at intervention does not work. Even if he relapses or does not get into recovery, you have learned these tools that can breed success over time. Keep in mind that these Behavioral Therapy (CBT) strategies are well researched and have been proven effective if administered correctly. I have combined these tools with those from Client-Centered Therapy, Twelve-Step Programs and Reality Therapy to present to you a strategy that has worked in my practice for many decades. Do not give up. You have to determine how to return to the model and find out how to do it better so that it will work. Sometimes we plant seeds that bear fruit at a later time. However, it is important never to allow his consequences of using to be rewarded or unnoticed.

As a result of your intervention, your child must see, at a deep level inside, a cellular level, that the problem exists in him and that it is grave. You can accept this if you plan the strategy with others and use an expert if there is any doubt. When all have spoken, your child can then reply. If you are exact, caring and sincere, he may hear your message. He has let everyone talk as agreed upon at the beginning. Expect him to respond with cooperation. You have connected with that part of him that wants help and helped him see that the problem is deadly, progressive and not going away ever. This is addiction. It does not go away. The next step is part 6, treatment entry.

CHAPTER ELEVEN

ENTRY INTO TREATMENT - STEP 6

Invest in the Solution or the Problem.
Doc Pete

Toward the end of the intervention, after he has talked, the most important question to ask him, the first question that will predict whether he will be successful, is, "Do you want help?" If he answers that he does want help ask him the second question, "Do you think you can do this alone?" If he answers "No!" he is now ready for recovery. It is our job to help him maintain this position.

Remember, in one week, or one month or sometime within the first year or two or three, he will no longer feel the pain of the losses and damage created by this problem and, if he reverts to old thinking, he will relapse. The opportunity we have now is to help him admit and deeply accept the fact that he is impaired and desperately needs help and cannot do this alone. This event can do that – It can help him feel the depth of his disease.

The above connection can occur if you probe by asking him why he needs help and cannot recover by alone. Help him to connect specific problems of his drug and alcohol use and give more examples of problems. Try to help him realize that, when he uses, he has problems in mental, emotional, physical, spiritual, legal, career, education, relationship, marriage, parenting, financial, and/or family areas. Many of these areas, if not all, have been impaired on a major or minor or moderate level. All in all, these problems are evidence that the drug and/or alcohol ingestion is causing problems and not peace of mind or continual euphoria. Making this is essential as it breaks denial.

The twelve-step programs help the person keep this awareness vivid in his mind as frequent attendance gives him both a chance to hear reality-based thinking about the devastation done and that still occurs and also see the reminders of the progress made in all life areas. Further, nowhere else can your son see the addict/alcoholic walk into a room looking like hell and having been to hell, feeling the pain of the recent damage done, talk about it and then heal? Your child gets to hear the problems and see the problems that are as elusive as time builds in recovery. This is why successful recovering people return often to the meetings and help the newer people. It's done at first because it's necessary to stay sober and clean – abstinent. After spiritual growth is attained, it is done for virtues' sake. It's the right thing to do. It is my belief that, when the addict/alcoholic stops 'giving away' his recovery, it atrophies until using or death occurs. Get to know these people. You will be glad you did. There are 'open' meetings that you can attend. You will be welcome. More importantly, attend Al-Anon. This is vital to continued success.

When the child is asked the above two questions and the answers are yes and no respectively, there is chance for recovery in the home and on an outpatient basis. If he does not think there is a problem, inpatient or natural consequences may help. If he is very impaired, insist on inpatient treatment. This may be the only logical choice. If he is still defiant and argumentative and refuses to cooperative, he probably needs to feel the consequences. Then your decision is either treatment or detach. If he has been to treatment you may want to do the latter.

If detoxification is necessary, use inpatient unless an M.D. tells you to try it at home. Many M.D.s will recommend a weekend at the hospital with medicine. Keep an eye on this as prescription medication is one of the three primary causes of relapse. The other two are overconfidence and resentment. Whatever the case, use treatment to eventually get him to what works: the twelve-step program.

If he wants treatment and needs detoxification, is in late middle or chronic stages of addiction, insist on inpatient. Research treatment centers (have this done already) and make sure they have a solid basis for their treatment to include individual treatment plans, twelve-step design, a family tract, a reasonable explanation for length of stay, an adequate staff, affordable rates, a good reputation and a good facility. Make sure that there are people on staff who have been in recovery for over two years and are credentialed with state licenses or certifications to practice treatment of addictions.

Most of the treatment centers cannot keep drugs or alcohol out of the facility all of the time. Make sure they have a policy and a mechanism to check on abstinence such as random urinalyses, hair analysis and 'checks' upon return to the facility and after visits from others. The program must have integrity and put treatment and recovery above or equal to the cost of treatment. They have to make money but make sure they have good treatment also. A good rule-of-thumb is to get a referral from someone you know who has been to the treatment center and has been successful.

A family approach is necessary as this is a family disease. As before, everyone is seriously affected. At times, the family members are hospitalized while the addict gets "relief." The family has no way to get any relief except for Al-Anon or counseling with a therapist trained in addiction. When he gets drunk or high and you get the hangover, you need treatment. Thus the title of this book: No Relief for the Family. There is relief for the family members if you do the best you can, do your best, and then leave the results to God. You can't control another. What we're trying to do is influence him with love and a well planned intervention and get him to twelve-step programs. The most effective action you can take is to go to Al-Anon, see a trained therapist, perform the intervention as explained in this book and leave the outcome to God.

Treatment Will Not Cure Your Child

If he wants to try this at home you can think about setting up the home as a therapeutic environment. Remember that this means you are going to sacrifice your time and money, energy and health while jeopardizing your family's health. An important consideration to be aware of is that the addict/alcoholic has developed poor habits, toxic thoughts and maladaptive behaviors that don't go away simply because he is drug and/or alcohol free. The lying, cheating, stealing, overconfidence with bad judgment and lack of inhibitions do not leave until the person is in recovery for a long time and looks at these character defects and takes action to rid self of these. This takes years of work. Treatment will not cure your child in 28 days. You cannot cure your child. I cannot cure your child. It takes years of continual and consistent committed treatment to address these issues and heal. The twelve-step programs and its people do this; they know how to arrest this problem.

So you can see that you're 'biting off' quite a bit by keeping him in your home. Make sure he enters treatment. As regards to recovery and addiction issues, the addict/alcoholic will not listen to people who have not been there because they have not been there. We listen to others who have been there for many reasons. We need to be with our own kind in order to see the gravity of addiction, identify, obtain accurate information, hear from others who have relapsed so that we do not have to, get and stay honest about our Program and feel the caring and concern from these people. Credibility is 'built in' as addicts are less likely to judge one another. We know and feel this. This provides safety in our relationship. So you must let him go and do whatever you can to get him to treatment without forcing him. Do this gladly. It is like getting him to chemo treatment. Do whatever it takes.

Once again, this desire to take care of the problem yourself is natural in any family but more so in a drug-affected family. Dismiss this and use logic. He will get better at these meetings by associating with these people. You will eventually be glad he's going. For this and many others reasons, the meetings are imperative. Help get him to meetings. This is the most important thing about treatment I can tell you. You may feel jealous or angry at treatment and/or twelve-step persons. Drop any guilt you may have about not being able to fix this problem. You can't perform the miracle; I can't perform the miracle; God can, so let Him. Your child will find God at meetings.

The Therapeutic Home

If you decide on keeping him at home and placing him in outpatient treatment, you can set up your home as a therapeutic community. This innovative mode of treatment was designed as a family therapy alternative. I thought it would be ideal for families in recovery. I like it because it places responsibility for the child where it belongs with the parents. It also involves using the parents as the therapists. This goes back to my original premise that 'parents are the first teachers and the best teachers and the home is the first and best, most effective, school. However, this is a great responsibility for the family. Be sure that your family is resilient enough to withstand the possible manipulation and negative behavior that is sure to be created as the problem is tackled.

The course of recovery in the first year is riddled with chaos, intermittent denial and an influx of random feelings and stressors that have been festering under the surface of the addict and the family for years. The problem is usually generational. Addiction is usually somewhere in your family. Those feelings and issues of miscommunication or non-communication trust and repressed feelings emerge as family members and these 'frozen feelings' begin to 'thaw out'. For this reason, Al-Anon is such a blessing. When I can motivate families to twelve-step programs, we succeed. When members do not go and use their old thinking, "I've got this!" or "I turned out ok!" They are using the same thinking that the addict uses when thinking about using again. Keep in mind that the family's connection to the addict usually parallels the addict's connection to the drug and or alcohol. When the family can get clear, humble and honest enough to realize this and work on self, they don't enable and now the addict has a very good chance to recover.

The therapeutic home is just that. It is a place where your child can stay that is different than the home where he used to live. He can have his room but there may not be a door on it. This, like the other rules, depends on your child's past behavior. If he has snuck others into his room, used in his room, snuck out himself, you may want to take his door off. You can also bolt down his windows. He can also sleep in your room but make sure you are not the ones getting punished. It's your house. Make the rules. Base the rules on his behavior. Let him know that he is in charge of his behavior and it is his choice as to whether this works. He has a choice to obey the rules and stay with you or not. Let him know that you are offering to help him because you love him. Help him understand that you are doing him a favor.

In addition, avoid being too fearful and overbearing/controlling. It is good to negotiate his rules with your partner and a good therapist who understands family addiction treatment. Take your time and start right with rules and have the courage to enforce them. The direction you takes will depend on the relationship that you have with your child, the level of trust and how 'far down' he has gone, i.e., how serious and damaging his consequences.

The Contract

Next, you must write a contract stating the rules. Put them in writing and post it in your kitchen in plain sight. Make copies and put one in your room and his. Again, be sure you review these with someone who has good sense and knows addiction. This person must understand the workings of the addictive mind and know that addiction is different at different times. Further, (stages of addiction) are different for people with different backgrounds and experiences but, in general, addicts/alcoholics have more in common than not (Tom Lepinskie, personal communication, 1997).

The Rules

Rules should be few, easy to understand, pertinent and measurable. Make sure you can tell when he's breaking a rule. Define and spell out the rule. Keeping your room clean can mean different things to different people. Write down the steps. For example, you are to make your bed with the pillows and covers and sheets tucked in and looking neat. The bathroom should have nothing on the floor except for a bathmat and so forth. Be able to measure and identify the rule.

Do not have too many rules. Three to four is usually adequate and keeps this process simple. Remember that recovery comes first. This will help him to follow the rules. The first and most important rule must be a rule regarding abstinence in and out of the house. Meeting attendance and adherence to twelve-step suggestions (As above, find out what they are by going to Al-Anon and go for yourself first and foremost) are next. Curfew is usually appropriate but not always. I have worked with families when the child was isolating at home and did not have a curfew issue. However, as he begins to feel better and wants to go out, this may be an issue. This is true of other behaviors and subsequent rules. As he grows or regresses, you may have to change the rules or modify them. For example, he may start talking with an old, using friend. You have to intervene and remind him that this is a relapse sign. See if he's still motivated to 'work' his recovery. Few addicts will listen and change unless they still feel the pain and loss of the addiction. If you take this pain away by not holding him accountable, you are doing the opposite of what works. You must hold him accountable!

Following the Rules

Few alcoholics or addicts will follow the rules unless they know that you mean business and they realize the gravity of the situation. In addition, use the whole team to hold him accountable, especially your spouse. Take this responsibility and back up your partner. If you disagree on an issue involving your child, talk privately and make sure you don't create chaos in front of your child. Always agree on the rules. Don't "waffle" because something else about your partner is bothering you. Iron this out first. This is the most important relationship. Try to deliver the messages about relapse as a team. If he objects, assume he is already using and have him drug tested. Let him know he has to earn your trust and his cooperation is one way to do this. Remind him that he has betrayed you and the family and you can no longer tolerate his addictive behaviors. This would not be good for him and it would not be good for you or your family.

Another rule is respect. He must display an appropriate attitude and behavior toward family. Work and/or school have to be addressed. If there is a baby involved address this. Financial accountability needs to be addressed also. Remember, all of these may not apply but, after the intervention, write the rules as applicable to your situation with your child and then show them to someone. Accept feedback, hopefully from a spouse, and make changes and alterations as needed. Keep in mind, however, that spiritual recovery has to come first, then abstinence, then the respect or job or school or health. Put off other areas until he stabilizes. Do not expect too much too soon. School and/or job are not necessarily signs of good recovery. Spiritual actions and twelve-step participation are.

When you have this list, have non-negotiable goals, e.g. abstinence from all mood-altering substances. Then negotiate mutual goals with your child. Once he has seen the goals as fair and agreed to them, you will be able to enforce them and will have less trouble with infractions. Have a talk about being 'set up' as the police because you are. This was not your idea. Make sure you understand that you are doing him a favor. You are in the position of enforcing boundaries but you are working as a team and neither you nor your spouse will let this deprive you of sleep or be criticized for being 'rigid' or whatever. You care enough to take on this role. Let your child know that you will do this but insist on cooperation and let him know that you will not 'co-sign' old behavior and resistance of recovery behavior.

Good Recovery

A good sign is when he lets you know that he is grateful and, more importantly, shows you. Believe the actions and not his words. Look for good recovery actions. You will see a desire to go to meetings, a change in attitude, conversations about recovery meetings, a sponsor, steps… When the family attends their meeting, there is common ground, a common language, common growth and a tendency to see recovery as a 'way of life' which it needs to be. Trust me; the family moving in the same direction succeeds. There will be a tendency toward humility and cooperation with household rules and responsibilities. He will want to go to meetings because they work. This involvement will help your child arrest his problem (disease).

There are other ways to get sober and clean if the addict identifies the issue at an early age and takes action before the disease consumes the addict. The action involves trusting God, making up for wrongs and omissions and being useful, preferably those who suffer from the same problem. The concern here is that the negative defects that are germane to addicts are addressed. The self-centeredness and build up of anger and fear, guilt and hurts do not vanish when the 'product' is eliminated. Damage has been done to the mind and the emotional life of the addict. I think that there may be a connection between serious criminal behavior and untreated addiction. There's an old story that's well known in the recovery world that relates, "When you sober up a horse thief, you have a sober horse thief." Another is, "You can take the rum out of a fruit cake but you still have a fruit cake." I know people who don't drink or use drugs anymore and practice being good family men, are churchgoers and work hard at their marriage. However, the emotional damage is apparent as there has been no treatment. Quality of life is a big concern.

Actually, I am open-minded to other ways to get and stay sober and clean but I have not seen this or read any valid and reliable research that is rigorous. I would like to know if there are other ways.

From now on your most important job is to hold him accountable.

CHAPTER TWELVE

DEFENSE AND MAINTENANCE - STEP 7

If something works this good, do more of it, not less and don't stop!
Doc Pete

This last chapter involves letting go, taking charge, going to Al-Anon (again, this treats the family members), learning what good recovery is, learning what poor recovery looks like, redefining your role, redefining your child's role as needed and learning about and then re-deciding what you'll do if your child relapses. This chapter serves in part as a summary of the previous chapters. Much of this has already been defined in the contract. The rules can be difficult to enforce but are vital to your child's success. This commitment to his success is real love.

The easy way out is to let the rules "slide" and be comfortable. When you look closely at this approach or non-approach, you can see that what you are really doing is avoiding the problem. Sometimes, it serves the purpose of 'buying' our peace of mind, avoiding the pain of seeing him suffer, but it really sacrifices him, 'sells him out' as he will continue his drug and/or alcohol addiction. We are ignoring the problem and solving our problem at his expense.

This selfishness will not help your child but will only serve to enable his using. Consequences provide the motivation to change. Hold him accountable or the disease controls everything and everyone. Treatment can reverse this. The addiction feeds on blame but flees from stability and accountable behavior. Throughout this writing, I have made an attempt to explain the disease, treatment and the addictive mind. The following should be easier to understand because of this. However, it is my experience that the real experts with the answers including identification, empathy, accurate information and direction are in Al-Anon. Join them if you want to be successful on an ongoing basis.

Most parents have difficulty with the concept of family disease. They see the problem as belonging to the child. This is difficult to explain as well as difficult to believe. Family disease means that the entire family has been affected by the problem. There is the alcoholic and/or addict and then the chief enabler (usually the spouse), the lost children, the comedian or mascot and the scapegoat (Sharon Wegscheider Cruse, 1986). All of these members take on roles to accommodate the problem and cope with the problem. Because at times the disease is barely visible, it is important to know what it looks like.

The disease is ever present but invisible in the home. The 'chief enabler' is usually the spouse but it can be anyone who ignores the solution and unintentionally supports the addiction through silence or assistance. This person covers up for the alcoholic by making excuses for him, telling the kids that, "daddy is tired and stressed" instead of "drunk and unpredictable." When the alcoholic is passed out on the couch, the chief enabler tells the family members that he is tired from work instead of passed out. This enables the disease, the problem, to remain secretive.

The illness 'splits' everyone and slowly contaminates the family until they become despondent and hopeless and become consumed by the betrayal and resentment, fears and blame, self-absorption of the addict/alcoholic and guilt for misplaced responsibility for the problem and so forth. The children develop 'roles' to accommodate the illness and to cover up the feelings of fear, guilt, sadness and rage. They do not make choices about their destiny but are 'programmed' to live with the effects of their upbringing in a shame-based family. The 'Hero' is perfectionist and usually stressed out to the max but makes the family look superior thus hiding the shame of the addiction. The Hero usually finds it difficult to have fun. The 'Mascot' or 'Comedian" goes along with the script, trying to get along and make the family seem 'fine' by being light-hearted. He covers up the shame and sadness of growing up in an addicted family. Like the other members, he hides the sense of shame and internalizes it and thus feels like 'lesser than' his entire life, being held back by his programming. The 'Scapegoat' acts out the feelings of rage and hurt by using drugs and/or alcohol or by getting into trouble in other ways. He has a lot of fun at the expense of others. The 'Lost Children' wander through life being controlled by their programming, giving in to the messages that they are not important and certainly can do better in life if only they applied themselves. No one escapes this disease. While it is true that some members escape from the home and set firm/rigid boundaries, they perpetuate the disease in their own families. Many times their family structures are rigid as they are based on creating the opposite of what they experienced in their family of origin. They overcompensate for the feelings and states of inadequacy by becoming very controlling, thereby sending the same or the opposite messages to their children who, in turn, usually rebel against the rigidity.

In other families, the disease is kept so quiet that it skips a generation. The parents saw so much dysfunction growing up that they did not use and kept this a secret. Most families of alcoholics and/or drug addicts are 'shame-based' and do not talk about their childhood because of the feelings of low self-esteem and the pain that they don't want to remember. Their children are not informed of the 'disgrace' and, if they have the genetic predisposition, are 'sitting ducks' for addiction. They receive no information on the disease and are educated by beer commercials and celebrities and movies that glamorize drinking and, at times, drug use. When they drink, they do not know about the tolerance so they can't notice when it occurs. For the same reason, they don't understand or even notice the cravings, blackouts or withdrawals when they experience them. So, as you may already see, the disease perpetuates itself from generation to generation. In the twenty-first century, I hope we are seeing the start of awareness and prevention of this insidious disease.

However, this problem usually has to progress until we can see these effects. It runs its course until we can no longer live with it or resign ourselves to keep quiet and let it pervade our home. We rationalize the problems and intellectualize them and thus do not stay 'in touch' with the reality that this problem/disease is infiltrating and ruining our family. Al-Anon can give us a clear picture of the problem and then we can begin to cope with it in a healthy manner. Uninformed, we are unarmed. We are unable to arrest it because we try to either ignore or control it. When we are informed, we are armed.

Magical Thinking

I want to caution you about a very lethal 'recovery trap' that occurs when an addict is not in true denial but denies in another way. He does not deny that he has a problem with addiction but denies that he needs help. You may see this during the intervention when he tries to negotiate treatment by saying that "he now understands his problem and he promises never to use again." This can return after he is sober and clean for a while. This thinking is still based on addictive 'magical thinking' and is usually an attempt at controlling things himself, the very attitude that keeps him active in his addiction. This is called 'white-knuckle' sobriety. Sometimes alcoholics and/or addicts abstain from all mood-altering drugs yet are not "in recovery." Sometimes they cannot stay abstinent. He or she is still trying to get sober without help. This is not the preferred way of recovery as the personality problems do not get resolved and may even worsen in intensity and duration. The co-dependent usually does the same thing. Denial takes the form of not treating the disease. Even in early recovery the addict and/or co-addict may think that he is cured.

Recovery is like walking up an escalator that is moving downward. If one stands still, he goes backwards. Anonymous

Priorities

Given the course of the disease in the family I hope that now, more than ever, you can see the importance of family treatment. The preferred way to obtain "quality ongoing" sobriety is to go to any of the hundreds of twelve-step meetings, obtain a sponsor (a coach) and follow the guidelines that are recommended. The twelve steps are worked by giving the sponsor permission to guide the recovering person through a series of actions which will alleviate the guilt, anger, and fears that have accumulated. A good sponsor challenges the "sponsee" with feedback and input that usually leads to an honest appraisal of the damage done to self and family instead of the old denial and justifications. This leads to further actions that lead to a contented recovery because the spiritual conversion has taken place. Actions will be taken to make things right with those who have been harmed, guilt is relieved and the person in recovery now has a new attitude and will be available to be of help to those in need. This spiritual path is nourished by continual attendance and participation in meetings. Without this, the family usually has an untreated person who is usually depressed, angry, sullen, and who still judges and blames others for his or her misery. With this ongoing involvement, all usually goes well. Sobriety/Clean Time is maintained.

Therefore, this path must come first and remain first. The recovering person must be introduced to this 'way' and then practice it daily as a 'way' of life in order to continue a sober and clean life. This will sound somewhat unusual as it is new and different from anything you may have thought would work. However, it does work. Believe me, it works. Over four million men and women, boys and girls are sober and clean today in the twelve-step programs. (If you know of a better way, please let me know.) That is a very strong testimonial to its success. I want you and your family to be successful and, therefore, I want you to go to these meetings and participate in the "program" of recovery on an ongoing basis. Make Al-Anon the number one priority in your life and then your child will be able to follow in your path, if not now, then eventually. "He will do what you do." If you make it a priority to go to your meetings and do whatever it takes to get there consistently, he will do the same. Remember, you are his first teacher. Teach! You can save his life with this approach. Without this, the family may not get better.

The Solution

This solution involves abstinence and spiritual, emotional, mental and physical growth. Twelve-step programs guide us through this process. Most counselors who have not studied addiction may not know of this or may not agree with these principles because they rarely study these concepts. Many see this as the competition. Our counseling training dictates that we take control. This does not work with addiction. Make sure your counselor is twelve-step oriented. If one is looking at 'hard' addiction (drugs and alcohol) then only a 'spiritual conversion' can arrest the problem. Very few people get sober and clean due to this need to control and fix the problem some other way. Letting go of the need to control is the key. We are not in charge of the addiction. If we were, we would have arrested it already. The disease makes us feel and act so out of control that we desperately want to control, take charge, and fix the problem. Merely obeying does not work as we later become defiant and rebel. We need to get sober and clean and take the suggested action because we know our way does not work and we desperately or, at least somewhat desperately, want to get into recovery. This is the mindset that works.

Good recovery is characterized by a lack of self-preoccupation and a desire to be helpful. Addiction is the "dark side" and just the opposite. You can't be on both sides. Good recovery is obtained by admitting the problem and then studying it and then 'doing it' by taking the necessary action to get and stay sober and clean. It is important to know that it either did or almost destroyed your life and that it's still going to try even though you're in recovery.

However, relapse can occur even when people are sober and in a Program. The MIND AND BODY AND SPIRIT must be and continue to be on a recovering path. I like the analogy that it is akin to walking up an escalator that is moving downward. One must keep walking up or go backwards - go down. This means one must have a vigilant approach to recovery, making it an ongoing regimen. A daily program is needed that includes repeated behaviors that are spiritual and practical. The word ritual is in the word spiritual. We actually have a spiritual experience that precedes treatment entry. This gets us to treatment. Most addicts pray at the end. Overcoming the self-centeredness, sick mind and craving body is not an act of our will power. We need a Higher Power to help with these. Our acts of will power and attempts to control our using are what keep us active in addiction.

Quality Recovery

At first, not using can be acceptable in recovery. However, as the person progresses in recovery, more attention is paid to spiritual matters, reparation and being helpful, humble and teachable. This is how self-esteem is built. When the addict/alcoholic works with someone who is new in recovery and is a part of saving that life, his sense of purpose is fulfilled, his commitment to staying sober and clean becomes enhanced and his self-worth expands. This is accomplished in a balanced way as the addict/alcoholic is convinced that God is involved in the change and the addict is an instrument of the change. He is then in a good position to improve on any area of his life whether it be education, career, job, relationships or health.

Now true friendships and relationships with family are possible. In good recovery, the recovering person's attitude will be cooperative and attuned to making up for past harms, especially with the family. New thinking will form as the person attends many, many twelve-step meetings and learns new thinking, positive thinking; thinking that counteracts the fears and resentments. Here he will learn to let go of resentments. Gratitude will prevail. It must be the cornerstone of this stage of recovery. Grateful addicts/alcoholics have a very good chance to maintain sobriety/clean time when they practice gratitude by giving it back, giving their recovery to the new person who needs them to live. This 'reprogramming' takes much time but it is worth the effort to save your child's life.

In weak recovery, you will see the return of most if not all of the old using behaviors that you saw when he was using. He will be 'relapsing' mentally or emotionally without ingesting drugs or alcohol. Usually he will eventually go back to active addiction. Relapse does not occur at once but begins with a different attitude and a slow 'drifting away' from recovery. My opinion is that relapse occurs with a negative thought process that creates actions or non-actions that were working. We have to learn to be positive. This attitude expands to gratitude and then to altruism. Now we are 'armed' with good recovery.

For example, I have not had a drink or a drug since my first twelve-step meeting. This is because I learned that I must be vigilant about recovery, putting it first on my priority list and embracing the twelve-step way of life. This became my new thinking. This has taught me to embrace the attitudes and beliefs that I was taught there. I attended three meetings a day for one year and still go four or five times a week. The more I go, the easier life is. The beginning and end of any spiritual quest is a sense of peace and I get that at meetings and through helping others. You may think that over a thousand meetings is a lot for the first year but it saved my life and was much less time that I spent in my addiction. My example is not a very good valid and reliable source as it is the experience of one person. That is not a very big sample for a research project. However, the hundreds of people that I have known personally and the four million plus who are sober and clean by this means are a good sample.

When your child stops going to their meetings, they are well on their way to using. They have stopped walking up the escalator. Using is inevitable. They may already be using and probably are. If you see this, have him take a drug test. Test for alcohol also. Do this quickly. You're in charge of your family. This is you taking charge. It is you being in reasonable control. It is an appropriate way to influence. Inappropriate control is operating out of fear and resentment, lecturing, blaming for little misbehaviors, not consulting with your partner, not talking about control and learning about it, not giving your partner permission to challenge you on your controlling behavior and your personal controlling 'pet peeve'. Yeah, you know the one.

Untreated Addiction

Now for a word or two on untreated addiction. This can occur as a result of a return to active use, or continuance of addiction or even without ingesting any substance. Usually, an untreated addict/alcoholic manifests many symptoms. In order to continue use of a toxic substance, one must develop a way to justify or think irrationally. This takes the form of rigid thinking (without logic) based on fear and anger, two emotions that increase while the person continues to destroy self and others. Help is not available because the person does not seek help although it is very available.

Self-reliance continues or returns in efforts to treat an addicted mind and body with an addicted mind and body. This does not disappear in abstinence. It appears in thoughts/justifications in other areas. For example, the person sometime thinks that she/he does not have to conform to rules, whether public or domestic. There is justification for the rudeness, abuse, borderline abuse, and self-centeredness. When late or late middle stages of addiction have occurred, the person often believes that his/her reality is accurate. Thus, apparent lies and deceits are rationalized and blame is often placed on the co-alcoholic who is so beaten down that she/he can actually believe that they are at fault. Without a spiritual conversion and amends along with a dedication to living along spiritual guidelines, the addict is "dry" and still not fit for companionship. The co-alcoholic can decide to attend his/her twelve step program, and eventually "unplug" from this demise. The co-alcoholic can decide to quit waiting for the addict/alcoholic to get better before deciding that he or she can be happy. It is a choice that involves breaking dependency on a lost soul, no matter how functional or attractive the person may appear, growing up and learning to enjoy each day of life.

Pay attention to signs that his daily program is changing. Any alteration will be a signal. If he is in outpatient treatment, he may be missing sessions. If he is going and you see regression, schedule a urinalysis for him. Read the contract. Remind yourself of the agreements. Check to see if he is compliant. Be vigilant. Do not let your guard down. He is counting on this. Don't do it! Be strong. He is waiting, hoping that you will 'give in' to his demands and manipulations.

Look for specific behaviors. These may include not only skipping treatment or coming home late but also may include a different attitude or lack of cooperation, judging or blaming others, being irritable or restless or complaining. This will begin to become evident if you look for it. It is not uncommon for him to begin to have thoughts based on defiance. These can be seen in terms of minor resistance at first. He may 'forget' to make the bed or be on time for a meal or even late for curfew. You may see him with an old friend who is using or at an old hangout. Usually you will notice more than one of these behaviors. You will see a pattern such as fewer meetings, an attitude of entitlement, irritability, complaining, sleeping in, and so on.

Behaviors may come in pairs, then three at a time. These warning signals need to be addressed. Drug test him.

Many times they can be 'turned around' at once if you or he catches them in time. The plan needs to be revised if your child says he wants help and still thinks he is an addict. Do this before he destroys the relationship with you and others. He will turn to his enablers for help with using if he is already using or planning to use. Do not be one. If he does want help, have the courage to adhere to the plan. Enforce consequences. As hard as this may seem, you must do it. You agreed a long time ago to do this. Stick with the plan. Do not assist the disease. Do not enable. Remember, if you let this slide, he will need twice the consequences in a year or two or even sooner. He will need more pain and loss. You are preventing this by enforcing consequences with a caring yet firm 'position' coupled with an explanation of your reasons. Remember to err on the side of caution. If you suspect using, assume he is using until you find out differently. If you see signs, assume he is using and drug test him. If you are attending your meetings, this will be exponentially easier to see and you will be more successful.

Again, because of the nature of addiction, the person has a way to convince you that he is doing well. Try to resist being manipulated with lies or evasions of the truth or diversions. This is your responsibility. Focus on your concerns. Don't let him defocus. One trap to avoid is dismissing the relapse signals because you don't want to see them. This is a form of denial and, again, actually 'assists' the disease. It is then that the parent(s) become the problem, oftentimes helping the child to return to rigid denial. Do not become the problem. As above, the tragedy here is that it will now take a much more severe series of consequences or one tragic consequence to break denial and get the child back to recovery. Further, this regression can cause stagnation in one's recovery wherein it can take months and perhaps years to get back to where the person was spiritually, mentally, emotionally or physically in prior recovery.

Be careful also not to look for enablers to co-sign your relapse thinking. This means that you have returned to a state of denial, relapse, and again are ignoring or supporting the addiction. The co-alcoholic can actually return to a relapse state. This usually is a foreign concept that the co-alcoholic thinks pertains only to the addict/alcoholic. However, your relapse involves discontinuing your Program and losing your peace, your integrity and your freedom.

Another trap is becoming 'soft' and thinking that your son is not like that.

You are reverting to an old coping mechanism that didn't work then and won't help now. Instead, pay close attention to the behavior and talk with your team to see if they concur. Look at the written contract again to see if he is breaking the rules. This will help you to be more objective. Once you are certain he is relapsing, plan a strategy such as you did when you intervened. If you have a therapist, call and schedule an appointment. If not, be caring, firm and ask about what you've seen. Explain what you've seen and stick to the original contract. When you've explained what you've seen, ask him to explain. If he admits to the problem, focus on the solution. This will have to do with him changing his behavior and not merely talking about what needs to be done. Specify the behavior and adjust. If he does not cooperate, enforce the consequences.

Your job is to enforce the consequences, the rules. First, ask him if he wants help. If yes, there are still consequences. Trust has been damaged. If no, the consequences become clear. You wrote them down already. Keep in mind that enforcing consequences is helping him. Not enforcing consequences is helping him to continue using and dying. See this clearly. Even if you feel badly, guilty, for enforcing the consequences, you are doing the right thing. It is a courageous act that gives him an opportunity to return to the 'real world' of sanity and prosperity. Even if he does not come around at first, you can consistently remind him of this opportunity by keeping the contract. Behavioral theory is very clear on this. As difficult as it may be to realize, at time of crisis consequences help a person change behavior. An addict learns only this way. At first, no other way works. Be strong enough to do what you know is right. Just don't do it alone and – "JUST SAY SOMETHING!"

Summary

I hope you have read this book in its entirety. It is my baby! My life's purpose is to help families love your child back to life. I wrote it with the hope that many parents would read it, study it and be able to rescue their child from the grip of this devastating malady that is ruining families everywhere. Families are the 'key' to arresting this horrible problem. Your family has the power and influence to help your child enter recovery. My aim is to show you how to channel this and help your children unlock the chains. My life's calling is to arrest this problem, to put a dent in it. I respect and admire you for your diligence in 'tackling' this disease and I know it's not easy but it is possible. It simply takes your cooperation and work as a student of recovery and then growing in a spiritual direction, working on your anxiety and frustrations. Then and only then can you successfully carry a strong message to your child. Thank you for reading all of the way through. My wish is that I've been clear and informative enough so that you can apply the teachings and prosper without addiction. I wish you much success. I hope you will join me in my quest and "JUST SAY SOMETHING". God Bless!

Doc Pete

Printed in Dunstable, United Kingdom

91907788R00070